COLPs Tool

SECOND EDITION

Related titles from Law Society Publishing:

COFAs Toolkit
Jeremy Black and Florence Perret du Cray

Complaints Handling Toolkit
Vicky Ling and Fiona Westwood

Cyber Security Toolkit
Peter Wright

The Solicitor's Handbook 2017
Andrew Hopper QC and Gregory Treverton-Jones QC

Titles from Law Society Publishing can be ordered from all good bookshops or direct (telephone 0870 850 1422, email **lawsociety@prolog.uk.com** or visit our online shop at **www.lawsociety.org.uk/ bookshop**).

COLPs Toolkit

SECOND EDITION

Michelle Garlick

The Law Society

Material in Annex 5A is reproduced from Practical Law Company with the permission of the publishers. For further information, visit www.practicallaw.com.

ISBN 978-1-78446-045-7

First edition published in 2012
This second edition published in 2016 by the Law Society
113 Chancery Lane, London WC2A 1PL

Typeset by Columns Design XML Ltd, Reading
Printed by TJ International Ltd, Padstow, Cornwall

The paper used for the text pages of this book is FSC® certified. FSC (the Forest Stewardship Council®) is an international network to promote responsible management of the world's forests.

FSC
www.fsc.org
MIX
Paper from
responsible sources
FSC® C013056

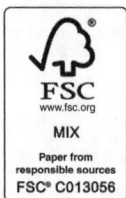

Contents

Foreword

While it is fair to say that many firms have been identifying and managing risks for a long time, the demands of the Legal Services Act 2007 and the Solicitors Regulation Authority's introduction of outcomes-focused regulation mean that all firms – whatever their shape, size or location – must prioritise risk management.

Instead of adhering to a precise set of rules the profession is now working toward a list of outcomes, supported by indicative behaviours, and this change in approach brings with it a greater focus on regulating the practice as well as the individual solicitor.

To help firms meet their legal and regulatory obligations, the Law Society established a designated Risk and Compliance Advisory Service. To date, the Service's compliance support includes bespoke in-house consultancy, webinars, monthly e-newsletters, master classes, seminars and conferences.

It is important for solicitors to be aware that they will not need to re-work all their systems and procedures in the light of the SRA Code of Conduct 2011. This is particularly pertinent for sole practitioners, who are often the senior partner, law firm manager and risk professional rolled into one.

With these things in mind, the Law Society's Risk and Compliance Advisory Service in collaboration with a number of subject matter experts has commissioned this series of hands-on toolkits.

These practical guides have been prepared with the busy practitioner in mind. They aim to help reduce the cost of compliance for practitioners by providing a useful set of reference notes, definitions, best practice tips and templates. Much of their content is informed by first-hand information gleaned through onsite risk diagnostic visits and interactions with members of the profession, and in response to practitioner requests for tools to assist in their compliance journey.

Our hope is that these toolkits rapidly become 'must-have' elements in every practitioner's compliance armoury and to this end I recommend them to you without reservation.

The Risk and Compliance Advisory Service would like to thank the author, Michelle Garlick at Weightmans LLP, for her contribution to the *COLPs Toolkit*.

Pearl Moses
Head of Risk and Compliance
The Law Society
August 2016

Preface

On 6 October 2011, the new SRA Handbook came into force. It marked a significant change in the approach of the Solicitors Regulation Authority (SRA) to regulation, moving from one which was rules-based to one which is outcomes-focused. There is now much greater emphasis on compliance with principles and outcomes, and also effective management. This is where the roles of the compliance officer for legal practice (COLP) and the compliance officer for finance and administration (COFA) come into play and whilst further changes to the Handbook are anticipated, the COLP and COFA roles are likely to remain.

The focus of this toolkit is on the role of the COLP (a separate toolkit has been published for the COFA) but there will undoubtedly need to be frequent communication between the COLP and COFA regarding risks, breaches arising and the need to report issues to the SRA.

Since the introduction of these two roles into firms on 1 January 2013, there have been some changes made to the SRA Handbook, some procedures simplified (particularly for small firms), more guidance given by the SRA and the COLP role has developed, thus prompting a need to write this second edition.

Whether you are a 'longstanding' COLP or are completely new to the role, the aim of this toolkit is to provide you with practical guidance and templates. Areas covered include the process for becoming a COLP, how to ensure compliance within the firm and dealing with your reporting obligations. We have also included additional monitoring tools and draft policies covering topics such as data protection, business continuity, complaints handling and file auditing.

Of course, every firm is different and one size does not fit all, but it is hoped that the toolkit will help you and your firm be compliant with the specific requirements expected of the COLP as set out in the SRA Handbook.

This toolkit is based on the law and SRA regulatory requirements as at May 2016.

I would like to take this opportunity to thank my colleagues at Weightmans LLP, in particular the Compli team, for their valued contributions to this toolkit.

Good luck in your new role!

Michelle Garlick
Partner, Weightmans LLP
May 2016

1 Role of the COLP

On 6 October 2011, the new SRA Handbook came into force. It marked a significant change in the approach of the Solicitors Regulation Authority (SRA) to regulation, from being rules-based to being outcomes-focused. The emphasis is now on more general, high-level principles and outcomes, which when achieved will benefit clients, as well as on effective management. There is also an obligation on an authorised body to have a compliance officer for legal practice (COLP) and a compliance officer for finance and administration (COFA). Whilst there are further changes to the Handbook expected, the COLP and COFA roles are expected to remain.

The SRA has created the role of the COLP to act as a direct contact between the authorised body and the SRA with regard to compliance. Each authorised body must be able to demonstrate how it is achieving compliance. This means that the COLP must have policies, procedures and records in place to document each step taken in connection with the firm's compliance and risk management requirements. In essence, each authorised body will need an audit trail to justify its actions.

The responsibilities of the COLP are significant and potentially time consuming and many will view them as onerous. The COLP (with help from the other partners/members of the firm) must ensure compliance is part of the firm's culture. It is not just about policies and procedures; the minds of managers, fee earners and support staff will all have to be trained to think 'compliance' at every step. Staff should also feel that they are able to report breaches to the COLP, be they big or small, and feel comfortable doing so.

1.1 The COLP's responsibilities

The responsibilities being placed on the COLP are broad. Furthermore, the COLP could potentially face personal liability for failing to implement a compliance regime. It is therefore important that the right person is chosen to be the firm's COLP. We consider who can be the COLP in **Chapter 2**.

The role and the requirements of the COLP are contained in rule 8.5 of the SRA Authorisation Rules for Legal Services Bodies and Licensable Bodies 2011 ('the SRA Authorisation Rules'), although, of course, the COLP will also need to have regard to the SRA Handbook as a whole (see below). Rule 8.5 is set out in **Appendix A**. To summarise, the COLP has the following key responsibilities:

1. **to ensure compliance with the terms and conditions of their firm's authorisation.** The SRA's regulatory arrangements include all rules and regulations set by the SRA in relation to: authorisation; practice; conduct; discipline; qualification of persons carrying on legal activities; accounts; and the indemnification and

compensation arrangements. COLPs must therefore be familiar with the general conditions placed upon the firm and its employees as well as any additional conditions placed on their firm's authorisation/licence. Ensuring compliance with the SRA Accounts Rules 2011 will be the responsibility of the COFA;

2. **to ensure compliance with statutory obligations,** e.g. duties imposed by the Legal Services Act 2007, the Solicitors Act 1974 and the Administration of Justice Act 1985;

3. **to take all reasonable steps to record failures to comply and make such records available to the SRA on request;** and

4. **to report to the SRA any material failure so to comply as soon as reasonably practicable.** In the case of licensed bodies, i.e. those licensed under the Legal Services Act 2007 otherwise known as alternative business structures (ABS), there is a duty to also report non-material failures as part of the annual information report required under rule 8.7(a) of the SRA Authorisation Rules. [Prior to changes made in October 2013, all firms were required to report non-material breaches. This requirement was removed for non-ABS firms following the SRA's 'red tape initiative'.]

Ensuring compliance is considered in **Chapter 3** and we consider the issues of reporting and recording breaches in **Chapter 4**.

Rule 8 of the SRA Authorisation Rules details the general conditions of authorisation including:

- ensuring compliance with the regulatory arrangements;
- ensuring that suitable arrangements are in place to ensure compliance;
- paying a periodical fee;
- having a COLP and a COFA; and
- in the case of licensed bodies, providing the SRA with an annual information report.

The COLP must also be aware of other specific parts of the SRA Handbook including, but not limited to:

- Principles 7 and 8;
- Chapter 7 of the SRA Code of Conduct 2011 – Management of your business; and
- Chapter 10 of the SRA Code of Conduct 2011 – You and your regulator.

Regulatory action can be taken against COLPs for failing to meet their responsibilities, although the SRA has said that it will not make the COLP the scapegoat and that ultimately the firm is responsible. It is for this reason that the COLP must be chosen carefully and must be in a position to carry out their role effectively. Whilst compliance still ultimately lies with the managers of the practice, situations could arise in which the COLP has to report issues to the SRA against the managers' wishes. A COLP must be given the authority to do this.

> Suggested wording providing such authority can be found in **Annex 2C**. This is not essential as the COLP's statutory authority is set out in the SRA Authorisation Rules. We have included it as some COLPs may wish to have the comfort of a signed authority from the firm.

1.2 Overseas practice

The SRA Overseas Rules 2013 now apply to those practising overseas and anyone affected should refer to these rules. It is clear that the SRA does not expect or require the same level of detailed monitoring, reporting and notification from those practising overseas as it would expect from authorised persons and bodies in England and Wales.

Rule 3.2 states as follows:

> You, as a regulated individual practising overseas or as a responsible authorised body, must monitor any material or systemic breaches of the Overseas Principles that apply to you or to those for whom you are responsible and report them to the SRA when they occur, or as soon as reasonably practicable thereafter. In relation to an overseas practice, a material or systemic breach will relate either to the character and suitability of an individual, the financial vulnerability of an overseas practice outside of established business planning, or a pattern of behaviour within an overseas practice that infringes Overseas Principle 6. Notifications by the compliance officer of a responsible authorised body, or by another person on behalf of an overseas practice will satisfy these requirements without separate notifications from each individual or body who has knowledge of the breach.
>
> For example, you will be required to:
>
> (a) notify the SRA, if you, or any of the partners, members, managers, solicitor employees or other professionally qualified employees in your overseas practice, are convicted by any court of a criminal offence or become subject to disciplinary action by another regulator;
> (b) notify the SRA immediately if you believe that your firm or your overseas practice is in serious financial difficulty;
> (c) provide the SRA with documents held by you or your overseas practice, to which it is entitled, and any necessary permissions to access information as soon as possible following a notice from the SRA to do so.
> (d) provide the SRA, if you are a responsible authorised body, with an annual return which:
>
>> (i) identifies the contact details of the office(s) from which you are, or your overseas practice is, practising, and
>> (ii) confirms that you have fulfilled your reporting and notification obligations.

2 Becoming a COLP

2.1 Who can be a COLP?

To be a COLP the individual must:

- be a lawyer of England and Wales; registered European lawyer (REL) or European lawyer regulated by the Bar Standards Board (BSB);
- be a sole practitioner, manager or employee of the firm or of a related firm;
- be of sufficient seniority and in a position of sufficient responsibility to fulfil the role;
- be approved by the SRA as the COLP;
- consent to undertake the role;
- not have been disqualified from acting as a head of legal practice (HOLP) as defined by the Legal Services Act 2007; and
- be authorised to do one or more of the reserved activities specified in the firm's certificate of authorisation.

The SRA Handbook Glossary provides the following definitions:

lawyer of England and Wales means:

(i) a solicitor, or
(ii) an individual who is authorised to carry on legal activities in England and Wales by an approved regulator other than the SRA, but excludes a member of an Establishment Directive profession registered with the BSB under the Establishment Directive [98/5/EC].

...

manager means:

(i)   a member of an LLP;
(ii) a director of a company;
(iii) a partner in a partnership; or
(iv) in relation to any other body, a member of its governing body.

related authorised body means:
an authorised body which has a manager, owner or sole practitioner in common with another authorised body.

There is no definition of 'sufficiently senior' or 'in a position of sufficient responsibility'. However, guidance note (vi) to rule 8 of the SRA Authorisation Rules states that the COLP's role is:

a fundamental part of a firm's compliance and governance arrangements ... The firm must therefore ensure that any person designated as its COLP ... is of sufficient seniority, in a position of sufficient power and responsibility and has clear reporting lines to enable them to have access to all management systems and arrangements and all other relevant information including client files and business information.

Who should be chosen as the COLP will depend upon the size and nature of the firm. The SRA has hinted that larger firms should think carefully before appointing their managing partner as their COLP as they may not be able to devote the time necessary to the role. For smaller firms and sole practitioners, the managing partner may be the only or obvious choice. See **www.sra.org.uk/solicitors/colp-cofa/help/ questions-answers.page** for more guidance.

Whilst the same person can be both the COLP and the COFA, that person must have the necessary skills and knowledge (and, of course, time) to fulfil both roles. The size of the firm, number of employees/branch offices, complexity of work undertaken and the firm's risk profile will all be factors to take into account.

If the individual designated as the firm's COLP has been approved by the SRA as a COLP for a 'related authorised body' (as defined above), then the COLP is not required to be a sole practitioner, manager or employee of the firm. This allows a COLP who is applying to hold the position in a number of related entities within a large group structure to make just the one application. The completed form needs to indicate all the entities for which the individual wishes to be approved.

If any aspect of compliance (but not responsibility) is to be delegated to others within the firm, the COLP will need to ensure that this is monitored and there is a clear line of reporting between the person carrying out the function and the COLP.

An employee can be the COLP (subject to being of sufficient seniority and fulfilling the other criteria). The definition of employee can include a consultant. Furthermore, a part time employee can be the COLP, again provided the SRA can be satisfied that the person can fulfil the role within the times they work and with contingency plans in place for when the person is not available.

A body corporate cannot be an organisation's COLP because the COLP has to be an individual manager/employee of that body.

> Firms should also think carefully about the personality traits needed to be able to fulfil the role of the COLP. A draft job description is included at **Annex 2B**.

2.2 SRA approval of the COLP

Part 4 of the SRA Authorisation Rules deals with the approval process for the COLP.

The SRA may approve a COLP if it is satisfied, in accordance with Part 4 of the SRA Authorisation Rules, that the individual is a suitable person to carry out his or her duties (rule 8.5(f) of the SRA Authorisation Rules). Part 4 of the SRA Authorisation Rules is provided at **Appendix A**.

ABSs need to have individuals appointed as COLP as part of the licensing process. Authorised bodies must apply to the SRA for the COLP to be approved under rule 14 of the SRA Authorisation Rules (save where deemed approval criteria is met – see below).

The COLP must meet the criteria set out in the SRA Suitability Test 2011 (see **Appendix B**) in order to be approved and the prospective COLP is under an obligation to submit evidence of their suitability to the SRA. Specifically, the prospective COLP should disclose information as to:

- offences involving dishonesty;
- offences involving violence;
- disciplinary findings; and
- disqualification as a company director or trustee of a charity.

The SRA can and may look at the honesty and integrity of those connected with and related to the COLP where it has reason to believe that that person has an influence over the way the candidate will exercise their role.

For approval, the SRA also requires the COLP to:

- co-operate in providing documentation and giving information; and
- provide a declaration that the information is correct and complete.

Until recently, there was no 'deemed' approval of COLPs (unlike the deemed approval for managers/owners fitting the criteria in rule 13.2 of the SRA Authorisation Rules). However, to assist small firms, the SRA will now **deem** a person approved as a COLP if the following criteria are met:

(a)   that person is an individual who is a sole practitioner or a lawyer who is a manager of the authorised body;

(b)   the authorised body has an annual turnover of no more than £600,000;

(c)   the SRA is notified of the appointment of the person as a compliance officer on the prescribed form, correctly completed, in advance of the appointment commencing;

(d)   that person is not subject to a regulatory investigation or finding, including a discipline investigation of which they have received notice, a disciplinary decision or a SRA finding, or an application to or a finding of the Tribunal, or any equivalent investigation or finding of another regulatory body;

(e)   notwithstanding the generality of sub paragraph (d), the SRA has not previously refused or withdrawn its approval of that person to be a compliance officer under rule 17; and

(f)   the person is not a compliance officer of any other authorised body.

The prescribed form for notifying the SRA of a deemed approved COLP is form FA6 and should be sent by email to authorisation@sra.org.uk.

For all other (non-deemed approved) nominations including where you need to change your COLP, the firm will need to complete form FA2 – Individual

Approval Application Form. An authorised individual manager should complete and sign the form on behalf of the nominated COLP.

The authorised individual manager must:

- provide basic and personal details about the nominated COLP;
- provide specific information about relevant experience, why the individual is suitable to the role as COLP, explaining how the person has sufficient seniority and responsibility and what training courses relevant to the role the applicant has attended;
- confirm that the individual consents to their nomination of COLP and the nominated individual must complete the SRA Suitability Test.

The declarations in the form are treated very seriously by the SRA so it is essential that all material issues are disclosed (even if the SRA is already aware of an issue) and that the declarations are accurate and truthful.

The form should be submitted by email to authorisation@sra.org.uk with any other necessary forms depending upon whether you are applying to be an ABS, an authorised body or changing the legal entity of the business.

If you are an existing business but the COLP is changing, you should complete the form FA2 and again, email to authorisation@sra.org.uk using the subject title 'Change of Compliance Officer' and include in the email the name and SRA ID number of the firm; the name and SRA number (or mySRA number) of the candidate to be nominated; and the reason for the change of the COLP. You should ensure that the person being nominated has a mySRA account before submitting the application.

The nominated COLP must not take up the role until they have received confirmation from the SRA that they have been approved.

> **The COLP Nomination Form is included at Annex 2A. There is also a guidance note on the SRA website at: www.sra.org.uk/solicitors/firm-based-authorisation/approval-colp-cofa.page**

The SRA has also made provision for the temporary emergency approval of a COLP in circumstances where the firm's COLP is unable to fulfil the role, for example, due to long term illness. In these circumstances, you must immediately, and in any event within seven days, notify the SRA, designate someone else to take on the role and apply for temporary approval. This can be done without using any form, simply by email to the authorisations team at the email address mentioned above. You must ensure that you give the reason for the application for temporary emergency approval.

Similarly, the firm needs to have contingency plans in place to manage the absence of a COLP, e.g. when on holiday or due to illness. The SRA guidance on this states:

Where a compliance officer is likely to be absent for any length of time they may need to be replaced. There are no hard-and-fast rules for when a firm will need to designate another individual to undertake the role but, by way of guidance, any absence of more than four weeks (including maternity leave) should trigger this action.

A precedent notification letter to the SRA applying for temporary emergency approval can be found at **Annex 2E**.

2.3 The COLP and the firm

The role of the COLP is still relatively new and unchartered and lawyers taking on the role, e.g. in a new entity/ABS, may not have had any experience of it. It also may not have been considered when the two parties negotiated their employment contract and/or partnership agreement. On this basis, formal provisions may need to be considered, especially bearing in mind that the COLP will be expected to report issues to the SRA even when it is against the wishes of the firm's management. The authority of the COLP to do this is set out in the SRA Authorisation Rules and some COLPs may feel that this gives them sufficient authority; others may wish to obtain the firm's management's written authority.

Some suggested wording for terms of appointment is provided in **Annex 2C**.

Depending on the size and nature of the firm, some firms may also consider obtaining a signed confirmation from each partner that they understand their personal obligations to comply with the SRA Handbook, that they give the COLP their authority to report breaches to the SRA and that they will not obstruct the COLP in doing so.

A suggested confirmation agreement from the individual partners can be found at **Annex 2D**.

The guidance notes to rule 8 of the SRA Authorisation Rules make it clear that the existence and the requirements of the COLP are not a substitute for the firm's and managers' responsibilities and obligations. Ultimate responsibility rests with the managers and owners. However, personal liability could attach to, and regulatory action be taken against, the COLP where they fail to meet their responsibilities. Firms and COLPs alike may therefore wish to consider including indemnity provisions for such circumstances. Such indemnities will inevitably be limited in scope, for example, perhaps covering financial sanctions only and will not protect against such sanctions as reprimands or, at the other end of the scale, the removal of a person's practising certificate or the removal of the person as the COLP.

Provisions for the COLP to have the right to seek independent legal advice at the expense of the firm and/or the payment of legal costs in disciplinary proceedings might also be considered.

COLPs may feel that without some protection, they will not wish to 'consent'. Director and Officer/Management Liability cover may be available and some professional indemnity insurers may offer an endorsement on the PII policy to cover defence costs for disciplinary proceedings. COLPs and the firm should discuss availability of such cover with brokers. Care should be taken to check any exclusions in certain policies. Firms too will want to protect themselves and ensure that they do not have to provide an indemnity when a COLP has knowingly been reckless or fraudulent or acted with wilful neglect.

The granting of indemnities is not straightforward and firms may wish to take further advice regarding this.

Finally, firms should ensure that their compliance policy runs alongside their internal disciplinary proceedings policy to ensure that all employees and managers are aware of the obligation to comply with the SRA's regulations, follow the procedures and policies of the firm and report any breaches to the COLP (see **Chapter 4**).

Annex 2A
COLP Nomination Form (FA2)

FA2 - Individual Approval Application Form

Solicitors Regulation Authority

This is a form to make an application to the SRA by an applicant firm or authorised body for approval of the following:

- Managers
- Owners
- Managers of a corporate manager
- Compliance Officer for Legal Practice (COLP)
- Compliance Officer for Finance and Administration (COFA)
- Related Entity COLP
- Related Entity COFA

Please read accompanying guidance on the SRA website: www.sra.org.uk/solicitors/firm-based-authorisation.page.

This form is **not** for:

1. Managers who meet the deeming provisions pursuant to Rule 13.2 of the SRA Authorisation Rules 2011, or

2. COLPs or COFAs who meet the deeming provisions pursuant to Rule 13.3 of the SRA Authorisation Rules 2011.

If you need to notify the SRA of a new manager, COLP or COFA who meet the deeming provisions, see the SRA website for more information: www.sra.org.uk/solicitors/firm-based-authorisation.page.

This application form is an editable PDF which you must save on your computer before and after completion in order to capture your data. Please include in each file name the name of your firm and the title of the form. For example "smith-llp-applicant-firm.pdf.

This form is not compatible with Mac computers, and data will not be stored correctly. You must complete the form using a Windows based computer. In addition the PDF application must be created with Adobe PDF, alternative format will not be accepted.

Section 1 - Basic Application Details

1.1	Is the candidate applying for a role in:	a new firm ☐ or an existing firm ☐
1.2	Applicant Firm name:	
	Applicant Firm SRA number (if applicable):	
1.3	Candidate is applying to be:	

☐ COLP   ☐ COFA   ☐ Manager   ☐ Owner

☐ Manager of a corporate manager; Name of Corporate Manager: _____

1.4   If an owner:

What is the nature of the interest holding? _____

Please confirm the percentage held: _____

Will the candidate hold these shares as a nominee?   YES ☐   NO ☐

If **YES**, provide details:

Section 2 - Personal Details

2.1	Forename(s):	Surname:
	Title:	Date of birth:	SRA number:
2.2	National Insurance No:	
2.3	Nationality:	
2.4	Passport/Identity Card No:	Passport Expiry Date:
2.5	Does the candidate have the right to work in the United Kingdom?	YES ☐ NO ☐
	If **NO**, please explain:	
2.6	Visa Number (if applicable):	Visa Expiry Date:
2.7	Home Address:	
	Post Code:	
	Email Address:	
	Telephone number:	Mobile number:
2.8	Main Office Address:	
	Postcode:	
	Telephone number:	Mobile number:

Section 3 - Professional Status

3.1   Is the candidate a:

☐ Solicitor of England and Wales

☐ Lawyer of England and Wales, please state title: _____

☐ Registered European Lawyer (REL) with the SRA

☐ Registered Foreign Lawyer (RFL) with the SRA

☐ European lawyer registered with the Bar Standards Board

☐ Exempt European Lawyer (EEL)

☐ Other lawyer, please specify: _____

☐ Non Authorised Individual, please specify: _____

3.2   Is the candidate entitled to practise law in England and Wales: YES ☐   NO ☐

3.3   If the manager or owner is an EEL, will the candidate be based entirely at an office outside of England and Wales: YES ☐   NO ☐

3.4   Is the candidate a member of any other professional and/ or regulatory body: YES ☐   NO ☐

If **YES**, name of the candidate's professional and/ or regulatory body:

_____

Registration/ membership number (if applicable): _____

Jurisdiction of qualification (if applicable): _____

Date of admission (if applicable): _____

3.5   Please provide a Certificate of Good Standing or equivalent written confirmation from the professional body/ regulator named above confirming that the candidate is:

- authorised by that regulator;
- entitled to practise (if relevant);
- not subject to any condition or other restriction

Attached with application form: YES ☐

3.6   Is the candidate regulated by any other regulator?   YES ☐   NO ☐

If **YES**, please provide details of the regulator including any registration number:

_____

Section 4 - Compliance Officer Information

This section should be completed for the COLP and/or COFA candidate.

If the roles are to be held by different individuals, separate forms need to be completed.

If your firm is nominating a COLP/COFA who is not currently regulated by the SRA, please ensure they register with mySRA and record their mySRA ID for use in this form.

If the candidate needs approval as a manager but otherwise meets the deeming criteria in Rule 13.3(b) to (f) of the SRA Authorisation Rules 2011, please contine to Section 5 - Employment.

Compliance Officer for Legal Practice (COLP)

4.1   COLP candidate is a:

☐ Manager   ☐ Employee

☐ Other   Please specify: _____

4.2   Has the candidate ever managed or supervised staff: **YES** ☐   **NO** ☐

If **YES:** Please provide details:

4.3   Has the candidate ever owned or managed a business alone or with others: **YES** ☐   **NO** ☐

If **YES:** Please provide details:

4.4   Has the candidate ever managed or supervised an office: **YES** ☐   **NO** ☐

If **YES:** Please provide details:

4.5   What past experience does the candidate have that is considered is relevant to the role?

4.6   Please explain why the candidate is suitable to the role of COLP, including explaining how they have sufficient seniority and sufficient responsibility:

4.7   Please provide details of any relevant training courses that the candidate has attended

Compliance Officer for Finance and Administration (COFA)

4.8 COFA candidate is a:

☐ Manager   ☐ Employee

☐ Other   Please specify: [_____]

4.9 Please provide a summary of the candidate's experience and knowledge of managing finance, including:

Billing and recovering:

[_____]

Computerisation:

[_____]

Preparing budgets:

[_____]

Controlling costs:

[_____]

Financial and management information:

[_____]

4.10 What experience does the candidate have with working with the SRA Accounts Rules?

[_____]

4.11 Who will undertake the day-to-day accounting activities in the Applicant Firm?

[_____]

4.12 Does the candidate have experience in signing off reconciliation statements? YES ☐   NO ☐

4.13   Please explain the process in the Applicant Firm for signing off reconciliation statements:

4.14   Please explain how the candidate will manage office and client accounts:

4.15   Please explain why the candidate is suitable to the role of COFA, including explaining how they have sufficient seniority and sufficient responsibility:

4.16   For firms who are not intending to hold client money, how will disbursements be paid?

4.17   For firms who are not intending to hold client money, how will compensation be dealt with and paid?

4.18   For firms who are not intending to hold client money, how will clients be invoiced and billed?

Related Entity COLP/COFA

This section is to be completed if the candidate is to be a COLP and/or a COFA for a related entity authorised body.

Rule 8.5 (h) and (i) Authorisation Rules relates to COLPs and COFAs respectively.

'Related authorised body' means an authorised body which has a manager or owner in common with another authorised body'.

A COLP or COFA who is applying to hold these positions in a number of related entities within a large group structure may make one application. This application needs to indicate all the entities for which the individual wishes to be approved.

The SRA retains the right to refuse approval in some or all of these entities.

4.19   Please list the related entities below:

Firm name	Firm SRA No.	Role COLP/COFA/BOTH

Section 5 - Employment History

Please provide details including length of time and the role type/title in respect of all forms of employment, including self employment, for the last five years:

Current or most recent employer

5.1   Name of candidate's employer: _____

SRA number of employer (if applicable): _____

Position: _____

Address: _____   Date employment started: _____

_____   Date employment ended: _____

_____

Postcode: _____

5.2   Did/does this employment involve the practise of law in England and Wales?   YES ☐   NO ☐

Previous employer

5.3   Name of candidate's employer: [   ]

SRA number of employer
(if applicable): [   ]

Position: [   ]

Address: [   ]   Date employment started: [   ]

[   ]   Date employment ended: [   ]

[   ]

Postcode: [   ]

5.4   Did/does this employment involve the practise of law in England and Wales?   YES [ ]   NO [ ]

Please provide details of additional employers on a separate sheet.

Section 6 - Business Interests

6.1   Will the candidate own, actively participate in or be connected with a separate business:

That will engage in legal activities: YES [ ]   NO [ ]

To which clients or aspects of their case will be referred, signposted
or transferred: YES [ ]   NO [ ]

Which are jointly advertised or promoted with authorised businesses
(including sharing a website, offering joint services or bidding for
work together):   YES [ ]   NO [ ]

If **YES** to any of the above, please provide details:

Name the separate business with any registration details for companies	Describe the relationship with the candidate	Give details of work undertaken by the separate business and if regulated, name regulator	Will the business remain separate or amalgamate with the applicant firm once candidate is authorised?

Section 7 - Suitability Test

All material information relating to the candidate's application must be disclosed. Failure to disclose material information will be treated as prima facie evidence of dishonest behaviour. The candidate must disclose any matters that have occurred in the UK and/or overseas.

If the candidate is only a manager and/or a lawyer owner and or the intended COLP or COFA in a recognised body or sole practitioner firm, they should not disclose any convictions or cautions that are spent under the Rehabilitation of Offenders Act 1974. They should not answer questions 7.3 (iii) and 7.4 (i) - (v).

If the candidate is an intended non lawyer owner in a Licensable Body and or the intended COLP or COFA in a Licensable Body they should answer all questions and disclose spent convictions and cautions but should not disclose protected cautions or convictions.

The Rehabilitation of Offenders Act 1974 (Exceptions) Order 1975 (as amended) was amended in May 2013 to bring it in line with the European Convention on Human Rights. The main changes were the introduction of 'protected' cautions and convictions. As a result of the changes, questions we ask about convictions and cautions do not apply to protected cautions and convictions. Failure to disclose such convictions and cautions cannot be considered as prima facie evidence of dishonesty. The Disclosure and Barring Service (DBS) will filter any protected convictions and cautions, so they will not appear on standard disclosures.

7.1   THE CANDIDATE HAS READ AND UNDERSTOOD THE ABOVE STATEMENT   **YES** ☐

Criminal offences

Refer to Section 1 of the SRA Suitability Test 2011 within the SRA Handbook.

7.2   Has the candidate ever been convicted by a court of a criminal offence:

    i.   for which they received a custodial or suspended sentence;

    ii.   involving dishonesty, fraud, perjury or bribery;

    iii.   specifically in relation to, or which they have been included on the Violent and Sex Offender Register;

    iv.   associated with obstructing the course of justice;

    v.   which demonstrated behaviour showing signs of discrimination towards others;

    vi.   associated with terrorism;

    vii.   which was racially aggravated;

    viii.   which was motivated by any of the 'protected' characteristics defined within the Equality Act 2010; and/or

    ix.   more than one criminal offence.

YES ☐   **NO** ☐

If the candidate has answered 'YES' we will refuse their application unless there are exceptional circumstances.

7.3 Has the candidate ever:

    i.   been convicted by a court of a criminal offence not falling in 7.2 above;

    ii.   been included on the Violent and Sex Offender Register but in relation to the candidates inclusion on the Register, the candidate has not been convicted by a court of a criminal offence; and/or

    iii.   accepted a caution for an offence involving dishonesty.

YES ☐ NO ☐

If the candidate has answered 'YES' we are more likely than not to refuse the application.

7.4 Has the candidate ever:

    i.   received a local warning from the police;

    ii.   accepted a caution from the police for an offence not involving dishonesty;

    iii.   received a Penalty Notice for Disorder (PND) from the police;

    iv.   received a final warning or reprimand from the police (youths only); and/or

    v.   received a referral order from the courts (youths only).

YES ☐ NO ☐

If the candidate has answered 'YES' we may refuse their application.

7.5 Is the candidate currently facing any criminal charges?   YES ☐ NO ☐

If the candidate answered 'YES' they must disclose the details of the charge(s). We will not determine their application until they can confirm that the charge(s) have either been dropped or the outcome of their case is known. Please attach all evidence to the completed application.

Evidence and rehabilitation

Refer to sections 7 and 8 of the SRA Suitability Test 2011 within the SRA Handbook. The detailed evidence requirements are specified after each section of the test.

If the candidate has answered 'YES' to questions 7.2 - 7.5 they must provide:

A)   a full statement of the event(s), setting out any exceptional circumstances;

B)   at least one independent report relating to the event(s) such as sentencing remarks;

C)   details of at least two independent professional people (of which one should preferably be from an employer or tutor) who know the candidate well, are familiar with the events being considered, and have given their consent to be contacted on behalf of the candidate for references;

D)   any evidence of rehabilitation;

E)   documentary evidence in support of their case and where possible an independent corroboration of their account of the event(s);

F)   if they were fined, evidence of payment of fine(s), reports can be obtained from the court.

The onus is on the candidate to provide any evidence the candidate considers necessary and/or appropriate. However, should we consider that the candidate has provided insufficient evidence, we reserve the right to carry out our own investigation and/or refuse the candidate's application if further evidence is not forthcoming.

Please attach all evidence to the completed application.

Assessment offences

Refer to Section 4 of the SRA Suitability Test 2011 within the SRA Handbook.

All material information relating to the candidate's application must be disclosed. Failure to disclose material information will be treated as prima facie evidence of dishonest behaviour. The candidate must disclose any matters that have occurred in the UK and/or overseas.

7.6   THE CANDIDATE HAS READ AND UNDERSTOOD THE ABOVE STATEMENT   YES ☐

7.7   Has the candidate ever committed and/or been adjudged by an education establishment to have committed a deliberate assessment offence which amounts to plagiarism or cheating to gain advantage for themselves or others?

                                                                        YES ☐   NO ☐

Evidence and Rehabilitation

If they have answered 'YES' to question 7.7 they must provide:

A)   a full statement of the event(s), setting out:

    i)   any exceptional circumstances,
    ii)   the extent to which the candidate was aware of the rules and procedures governing the reference of material or the use of group work or collaborative material, and
    iii)   the extent to which the candidate could reasonably have been expected to realise that the offence did not constitute legitimate academic practice.

B)   at least one independent report relating to the event(s) from the university or course provider, such as minutes from meetings or hearings;

C)   details of at least two independent professional people (of which one should preferably be from an employer or tutor) who know the candidate well, are familiar with the events being considered, and have given their consent to be contacted on behalf of the candidate for references;

D)   documentary evidence in support of their case and where possible an independent corroboration of their account of the event(s).

The onus is on the candidate to provide any evidence the candidate considers necessary and/or appropriate. However, should we consider that the candidate has provided insufficient evidence, we reserve the right to carry out our own investigation and/or refuse the candidate's application if further evidence is not forthcoming

Please attach all evidence to the completed application.

Financial behaviour

Refer to Section 5 of the SRA Suitability Test 2011 within the SRA Handbook.

All material information relating to the candidate's application must be disclosed. Failure to disclose material information will be treated as prima facie evidence of dishonest behaviour. The candidate must disclose any matters that have occurred in the UK and/or overseas.

7.8   THE CANDIDATE HAS READ AND UNDERSTOOD THE ABOVE STATEMENT   YES ☐

7.9   Has the candidate ever been declared bankrupt, entered into any individual voluntary arrangements (IVA) or had a County Court Judgment (CCJ) issued against them?

                                                                        YES ☐   NO ☐

If the candidate answered 'YES' it will raise a presumption that they cannot manage their finances properly and carefully, and we will refuse their application unless there are exceptional circumstances.

Evidence and rehabilitation

If the candidate has answered 'YES' to question 7.9 they must provide:

A) a full statement of the event(s), setting out any exceptional circumstances;

B) at least one independent report relating to the event(s), to include paperwork from the court relating to the hearing, with dates, court reference numbers and the outcome;

C) details of at least two independent professional people (of which one should preferably be from an employer or tutor) who know the candidate well, are familiar with the events being considered, and have given their consent to be contacted on behalf of the candidate for references;

D) a credit report, no more than one month old at the date of application, through Experian or Equifax;

E) independent evidence of actions the candidate has taken to clear any debts, satisfy any judgments, and manage their finances.

The onus is on the candidate to provide any evidence they consider necessary and/or appropriate. However, should we consider that the candidate has provided insufficient evidence, we reserve the right to carry out our own investigation and/or refuse the candidate's application if further evidence is not forthcoming.

Please attach all evidence to your completed application.

Regulatory history

Refer to Section 6 of the SRA Suitability Test 2011 within the SRA Handbook.

All material information relating to the candidate's application must be disclosed. Failure to disclose material information will be treated as prima facie evidence of dishonest behaviour. The candidate must disclose any matters that have occurred in the UK and/or overseas.

7.10   THE CANDIDATE HAS READ AND UNDERSTOOD THE ABOVE STATEMENT   YES ☐

7.11   Has the candidate ever:

   i.   been made the subject of a disciplinary finding, sanction or action by a regulatory body and/or any court or other body hearing appeals in relation to disciplinary or regulatory findings;

   ii.   failed to disclose information to a regulatory body when required to do so, or provided false or misleading information;

   iii.   breached the requirements of a regulatory body;

   iv.   been refused registration by a regulatory body; and/or

   v.   failed to comply with the requests of a regulatory body.   YES ☐ NO ☐

If the candidate answered 'YES' we will refuse their application unless there are exceptional circumstances.

7.12   Has the candidate ever been rebuked or reprimanded by or received a warning about their conduct from a regulatory body?   YES ☐ NO ☐

If the candidate answered 'YES' we may refuse their application.

7.13   Is the candidate currently facing any disciplinary proceeding(s) or investigation(s)?   YES ☐ NO ☐

If the candidate answered 'YES', they must disclose details of the matter(s). We will not determine their application until they can confirm that the matter(s) has/have either been dropped or the outcome is known.

Evidence and rehabilitation

If the candidate has answered 'yes' to questions 7.11 - 7.13 you must provide:

A)   a full statement of the event(s), setting out any exceptional circumstances;

B)   at least one independent report relating to the event(s), to include documentation from the regulatory/professional body, minutes from hearings and meetings, confirmation of outcome(s), appeal details (if relevant) and any sanctions;

C)   details of any disciplinary proceeding(s) or investigation(s) they may be facing. Please be aware that we will not determine their application until they can confirm that the matter(s) has/have either been dropped or the outcome of your case is known;

D)   details of at least two independent professional people (of which one should preferably be from an employer or tutor) who know the candidate well, are familiar with the events being considered, and have given their consent to be contacted on behalf of the candidate for references ;

E)   independent evidence of actions the candidate has taken to satisfy any findings and/or sanctions.

The onus is on the candidate to provide any evidence they consider necessary and/or appropriate. However, should we consider that the candidate has provided insufficient evidence, we reserve the right to carry out our own investigation and/or refuse the candidate's application if further evidence is not forthcoming.

Please attach all evidence to your completed application.

Any other behaviour

Refer to Section 3 of the SRA Suitability Test 2011 within the SRA Handbook.

All material information relating to the candidate's application must be disclosed. Failure to disclose material information will be treated as prima facie evidence of dishonest behaviour. The candidate must disclose any matters that have occurred in the UK and/or overseas.

7.14   THE CANDIDATE HAS READ AND UNDERSTOOD THE ABOVE STATEMENT   **YES** ☐

7.15   Are there any other factors which may call into question the candidate's character and suitability?

YES ☐   **NO** ☐

Unless there are exceptional circumstances we will refuse the candidate's application if they have:

(i)   been responsible for behaviour:

(a) which is dishonest;

(b) which is violent;

(c) where there is evidence of discrimination towards others;

(ii)   misused their position to obtain pecuniary advantage;

(iii) misused their position of trust in relation to vulnerable people; and/or

(iv)   been responsible for other forms of behaviour which demonstrate that they cannot be relied upon to discharge their regulatory duties.

Evidence and rehabilitation

If the candidate has answered 'YES' to question 7.15 you must provide:

A)   a full statement of the event(s), setting out any exceptional circumstances;

B)   at least one independent report relating to the event(s);

C)   details of at least two independent professional people (of which one should preferably be from an employer or tutor) who know the candidate well, are familiar with the events being considered, and have given their consent to be contacted on behalf of the candidate for references.

The onus is on the candidate to provide any evidence they consider necessary and/or appropriate. However, should we consider that the candidate has provided insufficient evidence, we reserve the right to carry out our own investigation and/or refuse the candidate's application if further evidence is not forthcoming.

7.16   Has the candidate ever been removed from the office of charity trustee for a
       charity by an Order of the Charities Act 1993?   **YES** ☐ **NO** ☐

       If **YES:** Please provide details:

       _____

7.17   Has the candidate ever been removed or disqualified as a company director?   **YES** ☐ **NO** ☐

       If **YES:** Please provide details:

       _____

7.18   Has the candidate ever been a manager of a body corporate which has
       been the subject of a winding up order, an administration order or any
       type of receivership, or has otherwise been wound-up or put into administration
       or has entered into a voluntary arrangement under the Insolvency Act 1986?   **YES** ☐ **NO** ☐

       If **YES:** Please provide details:

       _____

7.19   Has the candidate ever committed an offence under the Companies Act 2006?   **YES** ☐ **NO** ☐

       If **YES:** Please provide details:

       _____

7.20   Is the candidate aware of any matters which relate to the honesty and
       integrity of any person they are related to, affiliated with, or act together   **YES** ☐ **NO** ☐
       with which may influence the candidate's authorised role within the applicant?

       If **YES:** Please provide details:

       _____

7.21   Does or will the candidate have any arrangements, relationships or
       connections with third parties that may allow another party to have any   **YES** ☐ **NO** ☐
       influence over the running of the firm?

       If **YES:** Please provide details:

       _____

7.22   Is the candidate a manager or employee in any other business?   **YES** ☐ **NO** ☐

       If **YES:** Please provide details

       _____

7.23   Does the candidate intend to continue with any other business(es)
       if this application for approval is successful?   **YES** ☐ **NO** ☐

       If **YES:** Please provide details

       _____

7.24 Has the candidate been named in any complaints to their regulator
or to an Ombudsman in the last 12 months?   YES ☐ NO ☐

If **YES:** Please provide details:

```
┌────────────────────────────────────────────────────────────────┐
│                                                                │
└────────────────────────────────────────────────────────────────┘
```

7.25 Has the candidate ever been disqualified in any capacity under
Section 99 of the LSA or under the SRA Authorisation Rules?   YES ☐ NO ☐

If **YES:** Please provide details:

```
┌────────────────────────────────────────────────────────────────┐
│                                                                │
└────────────────────────────────────────────────────────────────┘
```

7.26 Has the candidate ever been disqualified from acting as a Head
of Finance and Administration or Head of Legal Practice by the SRA   YES ☐ NO ☐
or another approved regulator?

If **YES:** Please provide details:

```
┌────────────────────────────────────────────────────────────────┐
│                                                                │
└────────────────────────────────────────────────────────────────┘
```

Section 8 - Declaration

This section must be completed by an authorised individual who is a manager of the applicant firm. The
authorised individual must be authorised by all managers in the applicant firm to make this declaration
on behalf of the firm.

Knowingly or recklessly giving the information which is false or misleading or failing to inform the SRA of
significant information may lead to:

- the application being rejected,
- the application for approval of an authorised role holder being rejected,
- authorisation being revoked,
- approval being withdrawn, and
- disciplinary action being taken by the SRA.

It should not be assumed that information is known to the SRA because it is in the public domain or
has previously been disclosed to the SRA or another regulatory body. If there is any doubt about the
relevance of information, it should be included in this application.

The submission of this portable document form constitutes a proper application and the act of
submission is evidence of a binding signature.

For the purposes of the Data Protection Act 1998, any personal information provided in this application
may be used by the SRA to discharge its statutory functions under the Legal Services Act 2007, the
Solicitors Act 1974, the Administration of Justice Act 1985 and any other relevant legislation.

The SRA may make enquiries and seek further information considered necessary in determining this
application. In performing these checks, personal information given in the application may be disclosed
to registered Credit Reference Agencies who may keep a record of that information.

In making this application on behalf of the candidate:

8.1 I confirm that I have read and understood the guidance notes and the information in this application about the candidate is correct and complete to the best of my knowledge and belief. ☐

8.2 I confirm that I have authority to make this application and the declarations on behalf of the applicant and all candidates named in this application. ☐

8.3 I have obtained the necessary consents from the candidate for disclosure by the SRA to the applicant of the results of any checks of any information and any documents held in respect of any candidate. ☐

8.4 I confirm that the SRA will be notified as soon as any information provided in this application changes. ☐

8.5 I confirm that the applicant believes on the basis of due and diligent enquiry that each candidate is a fit and proper person ☐

COLP/COFA applications only:

8.6 The candidate consents to their nomination. ☐

Authorised Individual Manager

Please provide details of the Authorised Individual Manager making this declaration

Surname: _____ Forename(s): _____

Title: _____ Date of birth: _____ SRA number: _____

Role: _____ Email address: _____

Signature: _____ Date: _____

☐ If completed electronically please tick to say you confirm the declaration.

Section 9 - Returning the form

Please return the form, supporting documents and list of enclosures by email to: authorisation@sra.org.uk

Applicant checklist

To help us process your application quickly please check that:

9.1 The declaration has been signed and dated. ☐

9.2 If applicable, a Certificate of Good Standing from the candidate's home jurisdiction is supplied. The certificate must be received by us within three months from the date of issue and must be accompanied by an official translation, if not in the English language. We will require the original certificate of attestation. ☐

9.3 Written confirmation from the approved regulator relating to the candidate. ☐

9.4 Any additional information has been labelled and securely attached to the email ☐

Annex 2B

Draft job description

> **Note:** This is an example only and it will depend upon the size and nature of your firm as to the type of characteristics you will need the COLP to have.

Job title

Compliance officer for legal practice (COLP)

Role

- Act as a channel of communication between the firm and the Solicitors Regulation Authority (SRA) regarding compliance.
- Develop, initiate, maintain, and revise policies and procedures for risk management and compliance.
- Manage the day-to-day operation of the compliance programme and its budget.
- Direct compliance issues to the appropriate resources for investigation and resolution. This may involve collaborating with other departments and people, such as: risk management, internal audit, human resources (HR), IT, finance, the compliance officer for finance and administration (COFA), the money laundering reporting officer (MLRO), the data protection officer (DPO), etc.
- Monitor, record and report, as necessary, any breaches of compliance.
- Respond to alleged breaches of rules, regulations and policies.
- Remain up to date regarding the firm's compliance obligations.
- Identify potential areas of compliance vulnerability and risk; develop and implement corrective action plans for resolution of problematic issues, and provide general guidance on how to avoid or deal with similar situations in the future.
- Monitor the performance of the compliance regime and review policies on a continuing basis, taking appropriate steps to improve their effectiveness.
- Act as an internal resource with whom concerned employees may communicate and seek advice.
- Report, on a regular basis, and as directed or requested, to [the board/senior management] with regard to the operation and progress of compliance efforts.
- Work with HR and others, as appropriate, to develop an effective compliance training programme, including appropriate introductory training for new employees as well as ongoing training for all employees and managers.

Qualifications

Any person applying to be the COLP must:

- be a lawyer of England or Wales; registered European lawyer (REL) or European lawyer regulated by the Bar Standards Board;
- be a manager or employee in a senior position of responsibility;
- meet the criteria set out in the SRA Suitability Test 2011;
- be authorised to do one or more of the reserved activities specified in the firm's certificate of authorisation.

Required skills and knowledge

Any person applying to be the COLP must:

- have excellent knowledge of the SRA Handbook;
- have excellent knowledge of compliance requirements;
- be commercially aware, astute and proactive in developing ideas and solutions;
- have well-developed project management, time management and organisational skills;
- have well-developed persuading and influencing skills;
- be confident, assertive and resilient;
- have excellent interpersonal and communication skills (written and oral).

Annex 2C
Authority from the firm/terms of appointment

TERMS OF APPOINTMENT AND CONSENT TO THE POSITION OF COMPLIANCE OFFICER FOR LEGAL PRACTICE ('COLP') OF [*NAME OF FIRM*] ('THE FIRM')

The Firm's obligations

The Firm:

1. will provide adequate facilities and resources to allow the COLP to fulfil their obligations under the SRA Authorisation Rules for Legal Services Bodies and Licensable Bodies 2011 (the SRA Authorisation Rules) and under this Appointment;
2. will ensure that the COLP has access to all necessary information and will be granted the necessary authority to exercise effectively the responsibilities of the COLP;
3. will ensure that no manager or employee of the Firm obstructs the COLP in their role as COLP and that the COLP will have direct access to the Firm's [board/management committee/senior partner];
4. hereby authorises the COLP to report to the SRA as soon as reasonably practicable any material breach of the SRA Handbook, SRA Code of Conduct or other regulatory or statutory obligation which the SRA Authorisation Rules require should be reported by a COLP to the SRA and waives any right of action against the COLP for damages or loss resulting from any such reports which are made in good faith even though it may subsequently transpire that the COLP was mistaken in the belief that there was cause for concern[; and]
[5. agrees to provide the COLP with an indemnity for any [financial sanction,] [defence costs (including the costs of separate legal advice where necessary),] [or disbursements] arising from any investigation, inquiry or proceedings brought by the SRA against the COLP personally PROVIDED ALWAYS that the COLP has at all times acted in their role as COLP with good faith and with reasonable due care and attention].

The COLP's obligations

As COLP I agree to:

1. take all reasonable steps to ensure compliance with the terms of the Firm's authorisation by the Firm, its employees and managers;
2. take all reasonable steps to ensure the Firm's compliance with the relevant regulatory arrangements;
3. take all reasonable steps to ensure the Firm's compliance with relevant statutory obligations;
4. record details of and, as soon as reasonably practicable, report to the SRA any failure to comply where such failure is material on its own or as part of a pattern; and

5. record details of any non-material failure to comply [[for ABS only:] and include this information in the annual report to the SRA].

Signed on behalf of the Firm

_____

Signature

_____

Name and position, printed

_____

Date

COLP's consent

I hereby accept appointment as the COLP of the Firm on the terms set out above and confirm that I have the necessary skills and experience to take on this role.

_____

Signature

_____

Name and position, printed

_____

Date

Annex 2D
Individual partner's authority

I, [*name of partner*], hereby confirm that I will comply (and use best endeavours to ensure compliance by all personnel supervised by me) with all statutes, regulations, professional standards and other provisions as may from time to time govern the conduct of the firm or be determined by [*name of firm*] as standards to be voluntarily applied by [*name of firm*] including the firm's risk management and quality procedures. I also confirm that I will not in any way obstruct the compliance officer for legal practice (COLP) and compliance officer for finance and administration (COFA) in fulfilling their roles and hereby authorise the COLP and COFA to report any material breaches to the Solicitors Regulation Authority in accordance with the requirements of the SRA Authorisation Rules for Legal Services Bodies and Licensable Bodies 2011.

_____

Signature

_____

Name, printed

_____

Date

Annex 2E

Notification and temporary emergency approval application letter to the SRA

[*Firm's contact details*]

Solicitors Regulation Authority
The Cube
199 Wharfside Street
Birmingham
B1 1RN

By email to: authorisations@sra.org.uk

[*Date*]

Your ref: [*SRA ref*]
Our ref: [*internal ref*]

Dear Sirs

We write to advise you that our existing COLP, [*name*], is currently unable to fulfil [his/her] role due to [*set out circumstances*]. In accordance with rule 18 of the SRA Authorisation Rules for Legal Services Bodies and Licensable Bodies 2011, we are writing to notify you of our designation of [*name of temporary replacement*] as the COLP and hereby apply for temporary emergency approval of [*name of temporary replacement*].

Please acknowledge receipt of this notification with confirmation that temporary approval has been granted.

We look forward to hearing from you.

Yours faithfully

Annex 2F
Checklist for new COLPs

Action	Yes	No	Comments
Personal			
Do you comply with SRA suitability test?			
Nomination in?			
Received approval from SRA?			
Access to all necessary information?			
Considered need for indemnities from partnership/revisions needed to partnership deed?/separate agreement needed with authority to act/report etc?			
Considered additional COLP/D and O/management liability insurance need?			
Job description needed?			
Deputy needed/delegation? If so, are reporting lines clearly set up?			
Ensuring compliance			
Read and understood the SRA Handbook?			
Created/revised office manual?			
Identified risks to business? • Brainstorming sessions? • Prepared risk register? • Gap analysis prepared? • Prepared compliance plan?			
Staff training – do they know who the COLP is and your role/their obligations?			
Set up reporting format for key personnel in firm eg HR/Marketing/COFA/Managing Partner/IT, etc?			
Monitoring			
Controls put in place?			
Testing procedures considered and put into effect?			
Records for evidencing monitoring set up? E.g. Monthly compliance monitoring form			
Red flags identified?			
Reporting			
Whistle-blowing policy?			
Clear reporting lines?			
Internal breach report form needed for staff to report?			
Breach review/record of breaches form set up?			
Annual information report and changes to key personnel – diarised and person responsible for completion identified			

3 Ensuring compliance

In this section, we consider the COLP's responsibilities for ensuring compliance.

To ensure that compliance is enshrined within the firm, policies and procedures will need to be implemented, reviewed and monitored for compliance and then improved upon where necessary. The SRA has provided guidance on the systems that it will expect to see in place in every practice (see guidance note (iii) to rule 8 of the SRA Authorisation Rules and below).

Systems and processes should be proportionate as overly complex systems become unmanageable and thus ineffective or honoured in the breach.

The key to meeting the requirements of the role is to keep a record – an audit trail – of the steps taken from the carrying out of a risk assessment through to ongoing monitoring. This is particularly important, for example, when new sources of work or opportunities are envisaged. This record keeping will be crucial in illustrating to the SRA that the COLP has been fulfilling the role. It is important to remember that the COLP will not be personally liable for breaches per se, but could be liable for failing to implement, or for failing to illustrate that they have implemented, systems to avoid such breaches. In the author's experience of speaking to many COLPs, documenting/record keeping is the area, in particular, that falls down or is not done well enough.

3.1 Compliance plan

In guidance note (iii) to rule 8 of the SRA Authorisation Rules, the SRA highlights that firms should have suitable arrangements for compliance with the SRA's regulatory requirements (a 'compliance plan'). (See also Chapter 7 of the SRA Code of Conduct.) What needs to be covered by the compliance plan will depend on factors such as the size and nature of the practice, its work and its areas of risk. According to the guidance note, common areas which the SRA expects to see in a compliance plan include:

(a)   clearly defined governance arrangements providing a transparent framework for responsibilities within the firm;

(b)   appropriate accounting procedures;

(c)   a system for ensuring that only the appropriate people authorise payments from client account;

(d)   a system for ensuring that undertakings are given only when intended, and that compliance with them is monitored and enforced;

(e)   appropriate checks on new staff or contractors;

(f)   a system for ensuring that basic regulatory deadlines are not missed, e.g. submission of the firm's accountant's report, arranging indemnity cover, renewal of practising certificates and registrations, renewal of all lawyers' licences to practise and provision of regulatory information;

(g)   a system for monitoring, reviewing and managing risks;

(h)   ensuring that issues of conduct are given appropriate weight in decisions the firm takes, whether on client matters or firm-based issues such as funding;

    (i)   file reviews;

    (j)   appropriate systems for supporting the development and training of staff;

    (k)   obtaining the necessary approvals of managers, owners and COLP/COFA;

    (l)   arrangements to ensure that any duties to clients and others are fully met even when staff are absent.

The compliance plan should be used to identify and understand the firm's practice areas, clients, business strategy, etc.

Key risk categories will include (the list is not exhaustive):

- HR and people;
- IT;
- finance;
- business assets/property;
- regulatory;
- reputational;
- operational;
- strategic;
- economic; and
- competition.

From this, the COLP will be able to assess the areas of risk and identify policies and procedures which can target and reduce the risk of non-compliance.

Whilst a compliance plan is not mandatory (it is referred to in non-mandatory guidance notes), firms which choose not to use one must ask themselves whether and how they will be able to show that they have suitable arrangements in place to ensure compliance.

A compliance plan can take many formats and is unique to each and every firm, so providing a general precedent within this toolkit is not possible. However, at **Annex 3A** there is a draft outline of a compliance plan which includes suggested areas, topics and questions each firm should consider. An office manual setting out the firm's procedures and policies would equally suffice provided it covers all the regulatory requirements.

In any event, the office manual or compliance plan should be a live, working document which the COLP takes overall control of reviewing and updating. The COLP must also ensure that what is said within the office manual or compliance plan is actually done in practice. This is where monitoring, e.g. through audit and testing comes into play. Again, this is an area which in the author's experience is not done as well as it might be. The use of audit software can help with monitoring and identifying trends/patterns of behaviour or systems requiring improvement.

3.2 Risk register

Whilst again there is no obligation to have a risk register, Chapter 7 of the SRA Code of Conduct (at O(7.3)) requires that 'you identify, monitor and manage risks to compliance with all the Principles, rules and outcomes and other requirements of the Handbook, if applicable to you, and take steps to address issues identified ...'. Having a risk register will enable the COLP to do this.

COLPs should use the risk register as a tool to identify, assess and manage risks down to acceptable levels. Actions can then be instigated to reduce the probability and potential impact of specific risks.

The COLP should seek input from personnel from various departments (including department heads, managers and support workers). Different departments will face different risks which will have a variety of impacts on the department involved and on the wider firm.

The register provides a framework in which problems that threaten client services and the business are highlighted. It should give a snapshot of the firm's risk profile at any given moment in time and provide support to the COLP in his or her role to ensure the firm complies with regulatory and statutory requirements.

It is a key document in the firm's overall risk framework and a valuable strategic tool. It should not be something that is just lifted verbatim from a text book and left in a ringbinder to collect dust!

The SRA also provides regular 'Risk Outlooks' identifying high risk issues. All COLPs should ensure they read these 'Risk Outlooks' and assess whether the risks identified apply to their firm, react accordingly and update their risk register, policies and procedures and raise awareness if necessary.

An example risk register is shown at Table 3.1. The template is provided at **Annex 3B**.

In the example, we have used high/medium/low to evaluate the impact and likelihood/probability of an event/risk occurring. An alternative approach is to score each risk. The scores, typically between 1–5, are multiplied together and the results will help you work out what is a high, medium or low risk.

For the response to each risk, consider the '4 Ts' – Tolerate, Terminate, Transfer and Treat (see below).

Tolerance – these will be the risks that can be tolerated, usually those which have been classified as low risk or where the risk has an upside/advantage sufficient to make it worth accepting.

Terminate – this involves not pursuing a particular course of action as the outcome would be undesirable, for example not taking on a particular type of work as it would be unprofitable or the risk to the practice deemed to be too high.

Transfer – this involves sharing the risk and is usually associated with the firm's PII/ other insurance policies.

Treat – identifies that there is a risk but it can be treated by the implementation of policies/procedures, etc. to reduce the likelihood/impact of the risk arising.

Table 3.1 Example risk register

Note: The examples in this risk register will not cover all of the risks that your firm faces. The risk register must be individually tailored to your firm and risks considered in context. The risk register can be created on a simple spreadsheet or more sophisticated software can be used.

Risk identified	Potential consequences	Impact (high/ medium/ low)	Probability (high/ medium/ low)	Overall risk (high/ medium/ low)	Response	Action plan	Owner	Delivery date	Review date	Notes
Client care										
Client engagement letters:										
• Content	Complaints /claims/ costs recovery	High	Medium	High	Partners only sign client care letters having checked properly scoped and costed	Review client engagement letters to ensure compliance with outcomes				
• Not sent out		High	Medium	High	Reminder system in case management software					
Client dissatisfaction	Complaints to LeO/SRA	High	Low	Medium	File reviews	Monthly review of complaints arising				
Complaints handling	LeO case fees	High	Low	Medium	Complaints policy	Review complaints policy	COLP/ complaints partner			
Inadequate resources	Delay in service to client	High	Medium	Medium/ high		Review resources				
Inaccurate costs estimates	Complaints/ write-offs	High	Medium	Medium/ high	Costs updates to clients	Training to staff on costs advice/ estimates				

Case management								
Misunderstanding client objectives	Claims/complaints	Medium	Medium	Medium	Scoping of retainer and regular advice to clients	Provide training		
Failing to meet key deadlines	Claims	Medium	High	Medium/high	Key date procedures diary and back-up diary			
Non-compliance with undertakings procedures	Breach of undertakings – disciplinary and claims consequences	High	Low	Medium	Undertaking policy	Set up central register for undertakings	COLP	Monthly
Conduct/regulatory/compliance								
Non-compliance with practising certificate requirements	Unable to practise	High	Low	Low	Record keeping	Diarise key dates/liaise with HR	COLP	
Non-compliance with professional Indemnity Insurance (PII)		High	Low	Low/medium	Broker assistance	Diarise and liaise with brokers		
Conflict/confidentiality								
Failure to or inadequate check for conflicts	Wasted costs/loss of client	Medium	Medium	Medium	Conflicts policy and systems	Review conflicts policy; Provide training on conflicts procedures	COLP	
Conflicts arising	Cease acting	High	Low	Medium		Set up COLP authority record of decisions to act/no conflict	COLP	

Risk identified	Potential consequences	Impact (high/medium/low)	Probability (high/medium/low)	Overall risk (high/medium/low)	Response	Action plan	Owner	Delivery date	Review date	Notes
Money laundering/fraud										
Non-compliance with money laundering regulations	Exposure to litigation/prosecution	High	Low	Medium	Anti-money laundering procedures	Staff training	MLRO			
Data protection										
Non-compliance with data protection regulations	Breach of client confidentiality/claims	Medium	Medium	Medium	Data protection procedures	Staff training	DPO			
Loss of files, documents, deeds, wills, etc.		Low	Low	Low	Policy on removal of files	Staff training/safe storage				
Removal of files from the office		High	Medium	High	Policy on removal of files	Staff training/awareness				
Destruction of files, documents		Low	Low	Low	Policy on destruction of files, documents	Staff training/awareness				
Protection of personal ID, bank details		Medium	Low	Low/medium	Policy on personal ID, bank details					
Cyber attack	Client account loss/data theft/reputational damage	High	High	High	Cyber policy/procedures and training	Staff training/awareness				
Training and competence										
Non-compliance with CPD rules	Failure to maintain expertise	Low	Low	Low	Training and record keeping	Set up central record keeping	HR			
Health and safety										
Non-compliance with health and safety regulations	Injury to staff/visitors; Exposure to litigation/prosecution	Low	Medium	Medium	Health and safety procedures	Health and safety audits	HR			

Discrimination, diversity and equality						
Non-compliance with anti-discrimination legislation and SRA Code of Conduct, Ch.2	Exposure to litigation	Low	Low	Low	Anti-discrimination policy / Equality and diversity policy / Recruitment procedures	
Financial control						
Non-compliance with Financial Conduct Authority (FCA) rules (see Specialist service rules)	Disciplinary	Low	Low	Low	Registration	Check registered on the FSA exempt professional firms (EPF) register
Non-compliance with SRA Accounts Rules		High	Medium	Medium/high	Finance procedures	Staff training / Regular review meetings with COFA
Business continuity						
Loss of key personnel	Loss of income / Business interruption	High	Low	Medium		Locum policy/emergency approval of COLP/COFA
Catastrophic event	Physical damage to premises and client papers	High	Low	Medium	Business continuity plan	
Financial stability						
Market forces	Closure of business/expensive run-off cover	High	Medium	Medium/high		Consider merger partner/successor practice?

3.3 Gap analysis

A gap analysis means reviewing the firm's current policies and procedures against the principles and outcomes set out in the SRA Handbook. It is useful for identifying areas of weakness within the firm. Those firms who have the Lexcel quality standard will be familiar with the gap analysis process. A gap analysis allows the COLP to set out where the firm is, where it needs and wants to be and how it is going to get there, whilst ensuring it remains client focused. Be careful however of what the SRA has called 'unthinking compliance', i.e. a tick-box exercise, going through all the indicative behaviours of the SRA Code of Conduct (which are non-mandatory) without thinking of the clients' needs.

A gap analysis spreadsheet is provided at **Annex 3C**. Note that the SRA Handbook is expected to be significantly reduced in size in the near future with more focus on principles and professional standards rather than complex, prescriptive rules. It will move away from a 'one size fits all' approach by having two separate codes – a Code of Conduct for solicitors and another for firms – so that individual solicitors will be clear about their personal obligations and responsibilities, and firms will have clarity about the systems and controls they need to provide good legal services for consumers and the public. The gap analysis provided is based on the current Handbook but even after the changes are implemented, it is anticipated that it should still be a useful tool to enable you to identify the risks to your business.

3.4 Regular monitoring by the COLP

COLPs should also carry out regular reviews of compliance including a monthly review of the risk register and document their findings.

A suggested monthly compliance monitoring form is provided at **Annex 3D**.

The COLP should identify those members of the firm who will be relied on to report issues which the COLP will need to know about. These are likely to include internal heads of the following departments or those responsible for the following (unless the COLP is wearing all the various hats!):

- COFA;
- complaints partner;
- HR;
- IT;
- marketing;
- practice manager;
- practice areas/business lines/board/managing partner;

- data protection/information security (if not the COLP);
- money laundering reporting officer (MLRO);
- anti-bribery officer;
- audit team.

Monthly reporting from these various sources will be necessary in order to identify trends or patterns which require reporting to the SRA, and will also help to identify areas needing improvement and staff training requirements. It creates the audit trail necessary to establish that you, as COLP, have your finger on the pulse of the business.

A COLP may also want to consider obtaining feedback from the fee earners and support staff on a regular basis whether that is by an automated survey or questionnaire process in which the fee earners declare that they know of no issues or breaches, etc. (this can also be used to test their knowledge of the relevant processes/policies) or by providing, on the front page of the intranet site, an option for sending notifications of issues or suggestions for improvements, etc.

A COLP may also find it useful to have a diary or checklist of risk areas to review – whether they be monthly, quarterly or annually.

A checklist of routine compliance monitoring activities is provided at **Annex 3E**. This checklist can be presented in two formats, (a) by activity and (b) by regularity/frequency. An example of format (a) is included in this book; precedents for both (a) and (b) formats can be found on the disk.

A template Key Staff Monthly Report is provided at **Annex 3F**.

A template for recording reviews with the complaints/claims partner is provided at **Annex 3G**.

Annex 3A
Draft compliance plan

> **Note:** This narrative form is just one example of how a compliance plan can be presented. It should be used to direct the firm's staff to relevant existing procedures and systems, either via links (if the plan is on the intranet) or by reference to page numbers within an office or risk manual. It will also need to tie in with the firm's risk register.

[*Name of firm*]'s statement of compliance

In October 2011, the Solicitors Regulation Authority (SRA) introduced the SRA Handbook. To ensure compliance with the principles, outcomes and other requirements of the new SRA Handbook, as well as with our statutory obligations, appropriate systems and controls are in place. This compliance plan sets out the firm's commitment to ensuring compliance and provides staff members with an overview of the policies and procedures that are in place to identify, monitor and manage risks.

Risk profile

History and ownership of the firm

[*Brief overview of when the firm was set up and the structure of the firm. It may be helpful to include an organisational chart illustrating firm reporting lines.*]

Strategic objectives of the firm

[*Brief overview of the firm's strategy and targets, as these will have a bearing on the risks it will face. For example, the quicker a firm intends to grow the more susceptible it will be to risk.*]

Size of firm

[*Number of partners, employees, etc.*]

Type of work, firm's markets and client base

[*Summary of the departments and the clients of the firm, e.g. sophisticated and/or unsophisticated users of legal services.*]

Level of risk for work

[Low/Medium/High]

The firm's locations

[*e.g. foreign jurisdictions, multiple locations within England and Wales, High Street, legal aid practice, etc.*]

Quality/make-up of staff

[*e.g. level/types of qualifications, etc. – some levels/types may require increased supervision.*]

Work within regulated and/or unregulated sectors

[*i.e. for the purposes of the Money Laundering Regulations 2007.*]

Managing the business

Governance structure

[*What structure is in place to manage the firm? What does the firm have in place in the way of boards, committees or individual roles? What reporting lines are in place? Confirmation that issues of conduct are given appropriate weight in decisions the firm takes, whether on client matters or firm-based issues such as funding.*]

Business plan

[*Overview of the firm's business plan and its connection with risk and compliance.*]

Managing compliance

[*Refer to and identify the COLP. How is risk managed within the firm? What procedures and policies are in place? Where can policies and procedures be located? How is compliance monitored? Who is trained in compliance? Who can employees ask to seek training? Who is responsible for the management of risk? Who is responsible for ensuring regulatory deadlines are not missed? Who is responsible for obtaining approvals of managers/owners, COLP and COFA?*]

Financial management

[*Refer to and identify the COFA. Who is responsible for managing the financial risks? What procedures and policies are in place for managing financial risk? What accounting procedures are in place? Who can authorise payments from client account?*]

Training

[*Who is responsible for training employees? This may be several people, covering e.g. complaints, money laundering, data protection, SRA Accounts Rules, CPD. What induction training do you give? What training and development plans are in place?*]

Supervision

[*What supervision procedures are in place? Include reference to day-to-day supervision, file review and audit procedures.*]

HR

[*What procedures are in place to carry out appropriate checks on new staff and contractors? What health and safety procedures does the firm have? What arrangements are in place to ensure that duties to clients and others are fully met even when staff are absent?*]

Undertakings

[*What policy is in place to ensure that undertakings are only given when intended and that compliance with them is monitored and enforced?*]

Compliance obligations

[*Name of firm*] is committed to ensuring compliance with regulatory requirements and managing risk. Failure to comply with regulatory requirements can have serious consequences such as:

- clients not receiving the level of service to which they are entitled (for example, where the firm fails to meet their expectations), which may result in client complaints and negligence claims;
- damage to our reputation;
- the firm and/or individuals opening themselves up to being disciplined by the SRA or another regulator, which could result in fines and/or disqualification;
- the firm and/or individuals exposing themselves to criminal prosecution.

The firm has an open door policy and encourages its employees to share their thoughts and feelings regarding compliance. Employees are under an obligation to report any breaches of compliance to the COLP.

All employees have responsibility for managing their own risk and compliance. All employees must ensure they are familiar with this compliance plan.

The firm's compliance plan is constantly under review. The COLP is responsible for changes to it and any changes will be communicated to all staff.

The firm's compliance obligations are broad and include but are not limited to the:

- SRA Code of Conduct 2011;
- SRA Accounts Rules 2011;
- Money Laundering Regulations 2007;
- Data Protection Act 1998;
- Bribery Act 2010;
- Financial Services Act 2000; and
- health and safety regulations.

Documents supporting the compliance plan

[*It is likely that you will wish to limit access to some or all of the following documents rather than making them accessible to all staff.*]

- Risk register (located at [page [ ]/*insert link*])
    - Reviewed and updated by the COLP annually.

- Gap analysis (located at [page [ ]/*insert link*])
    - Reviewed and updated by the COLP annually.

- Monthly compliance monitoring form with supporting reports from [list of those from whom COLP seeks regular monthly feedback] (located at [page [ ]/ *insert link*])
    - Completed by the COLP once a month.

- Business continuity plan (located at [page [ ]/*insert link*])
    - Reviewed and updated by the COLP annually.

- Record of COLP and complaints partner meetings (located at [page [ ]/*insert link*])
    - Monthly meetings to review complaints.
    - Meetings recorded by the COLP.

- Audit findings

- Breach report form (located at [page [ ]/*insert link*])
    - Completed and submitted by any employee to the COLP upon realising a breach of compliance has occurred.

- Breach register (located at [page [ ]/*insert link*])
    - Updated by the COLP every time he/she is notified of a breach.

- Breach review form (located at [page [ ]/*insert link*])
    - Completed by the COLP once a month.
    - Reviewed by the COLP annually and updated as he/she sees fit to ensure its effectiveness.

- Record of reports submitted to the SRA (located at [page [ ]/*insert link*])
    - Updated by the COLP every time he/she submits a breach report to the SRA.

- Whistle-blowing policy (located at [page [ ]/*insert link*])
    - Reviewed and updated by the COLP annually.

Failure to follow compliance plan

The firm is under an obligation to notify the SRA of all [material]* breaches of compliance. The firm takes this obligation seriously and, as such, has implemented policies and procedures to ensure compliance. [Such policies can be found at [page [ ]/*insert link*].] Where compliance is not achieved, we also have a policy to notify the COLP of the breach. Failure to comply with the firm's compliance plan and its policies and procedures is a disciplinary offence and will be dealt with under the firm's disciplinary procedure.

Review

To ensure that the compliance plan remains up to date and effective, this policy will be formally reviewed every year by the COLP.

Signed: [*Signature of COLP*] _____

Position: _____

Date: _____

---

* Delete [material] if not an ABS.

Annex 3B

Risk register

Note: This risk register is provided on the CD-Rom which accompanies this toolkit as a Microsoft Excel spreadsheet. We recommend that each department completes its own risk register, with the COLP taking overall control. The spreadsheet includes tabs for the following departments: compliance; the board; finance; HR; marketing; IT and the various business lines/practice areas. It can then be adapted to suit the firm's business needs.

Risk identified	Potential con-sequences	Impact (high/ medium/ low)	Probability (high/ medium/ low)	Overall risk (high/ medium/ low)	Response	Action plan	Owner	Delivery date	Review date	Notes

Annex 3C

Compliance gap analysis

Note: This is an example gap analysis only. You and your firm must decide what aspects of your business need to be analysed. We provide the following headings as suggestions only.

	Do you understand the requirements sufficiently?	What further work/help is required to reach an understanding?	Do you currently meet this requirement?	Where are you short on this requirement?	Action required to address any gap	When do you envisage you will be able to meet this requirement?	Who will be responsible for actions on this requirement?	Estimated time required to address gap	Level of resource needed to address gap
SRA Code of Conduct 2011									
Chapter 1: Client care									
Chapter 2: Equality and diversity									
Chapter 3: Conflicts of interests									
Chapter 4: Confidentiality and disclosure									
Chapter 5: Your client and the court									
Chapter 6: Your client and introductions to third parties									
Chapter 7: Management of your business									
Chapter 8: Publicity									
Chapter 9: Fee sharing and referrals									
Chapter 10: You and your regulator									
Chapter 11: Relations with third parties									
Chapter 12: Separate businesses									
Regulatory compliance									
Practising certificate requirements									
Professional Indemnity Insurance (PII)									

SRA Authorisation Rules 2011									
Internal audits									
External audits									
Statutory compliance									
Money Laundering Regulations 2007									
Data Protection Act 1998									
Legal Services Act 2007									
Discrimination, equality and diversity policy									
Health and safety policy									
Bribery Act 2010									
Consumer Contracts (Information, Cancellation and Additional Charges) Regulations 2013									
Financial control									
Financial Conduct Authority (FCA) rules									
SRA Accounts Rules 2011									
Business continuity									
Contingency plan for loss of key personnel									
Contingency plan for catastrophic event									
Governance									
Governance framework									
Training requirements									
CPD requirements									
Trainee requirements									

Annex 3D
Monthly compliance monitoring form

Month of review:	
Name of reviewer:	
Overview of financial reports – cash flow; fees; credit control:	
Complaints:	
Client feedback:	
Risk issues – high risk matters; claims; circumstances:	
File reviews and audits – significant findings:	
Undertakings:	
Equality and diversity; anti-discrimination:	
Health and safety:	
IT security, cyber and data protection:	
Referral arrangements:	
Training:	
Business continuity testing:	

Signed: _[signature of COLP]_

Dated: _____

Annex 3E

Checklist of routine compliance activities

	Activity
Weekly	**COLP Obligations/General Risk Management**
	1. Review SRA website for updates/consultations/'Risk Outlook' thematic risks.
Monthly	**COLP Obligations/General Risk Management**
	1. Review reports from key staff.
	2. Review breach reports and update register of breaches.
	3. Check Law Society Practice Notes for updates.
	Insurance
	1. Review claims and circumstances.
	Complaints Handling
	1. Review complaints (with complaints partner if appropriate).
	Billing/Collection/Financial Stability
	1. Review with COFA.
	Anti Bribery
	1. Review Gifts Register.
	Data Protection/Information Security and Confidentiality
	1. Review breaches record (with Data Protection Officer if applicable).
	2. Review IT security and cyber risks.
	Staff
	1. Review issues with HR.
Quarterly	**Authorisation/Governance**
	1. Check 'Find a Solicitor' website for accuracy.
	COLP Obligations/General Risk Management
	1. Review Risk Register.
	2. Review file audit outcomes for trends.
	Insurance
	1. Obtain declarations from staff of any/no circumstances to notify.
	Client Inception/Engagement/Service/Delivery
	1. Work sources – check referral arrangements.
	2. Undertakings register review (if kept).
	Billing/Collection/Financial Stability
	1. Financial stability review.

	Activity
6 Monthly	**Authorisation/Governance**
	1. PSC Register updated?
	Client Inception/Engagement/Service/Delivery
	1. Review funding arrangements/costs info/financial benefits.
	Complaints Handling
	1. Review complaints for trends/training needs, etc.
	Financial Services
	1. Review mediation activity compliance.
	Independence
	1. Monitor for group contagion.
	Training
	1. Review list of staff who have not completed required training.
Annually	**Authorisation/Governance**
	1. Check conditions of licence/authorisation/waivers.
	2. Equality and diversity data.
	3. Notifications/reports to SRA re PC renewal.
	COLP Obligations/General Risk Management
	1. Review Compliance Plan.
	2. Review file audit process.
	Insurance
	1. Renew PII/other insurances.
	2. Monitor level of cover needed/top up.
	3. Check limitation of liability.
	Client Inception/Engagement/Service/Delivery
	1. Conflict checks – review policies and procedure.
	2. Due diligence/AML – review policies/procedures.
	3. Review client take on procedures.
	4. Client care – review engagement letter/Terms of Business.
	5. Vulnerable clients – review policy/procedures.
	6. Supervision procedure and policy review.
	7. Key date procedure review.
	8. Undertakings policy.
	Complaints Handling
	1. Complaints policy review.
	Billing/Collection/Financial Stability
	1. Check bill wording for compliance/TT fees/secret profits.
	File Closure/Archiving/Destruction
	1. Review policy and procedure.

	Activity
Annually	**Anti Bribery/Fraud**
	1. Review policy.
	2. Review Fraud Policy.
	Data Protection/Information Security and Confidentiality
	1. Review policies.
	2. Check ICO registration.
	3. Review subject access request policy/procedure.
	Publicity
	1. Review website, letterhead, email footer, list of partners, etc. for compliance/accuracy/not misleading/no cold calling, etc.
	Equality and Diversity
	1. Review/provide training.
	2. Review policies.
	Outsourcing
	1. Review arrangements/written agreements and standards of service.
	Financial Services
	1. Check EPF Register.
	Independence
	1. Review/monitor independence. e.g. third party/referrer relationships.
	2. Review separate business compliance (if appropriate).
	Staff
	1. Review policy for new employee checks.
	2. Review whistle-blowing policy.
	Business Continuity
	1. Review policies.
	2. Test procedures.
	3. Succession planning review.
	Training
	1. Review training programme.
Every 2 years	**Equality and Diversity**
	1. Complete SRA diversity/reporting survey.

Annex 3F
Key staff monthly report template

Date of report:	
From (name):	
Area of business (tick as appropriate):	Board Finance/COFA HR Marketing IT Complaints Partner Practice Manager Audit Data Protection Officer MLRO Anti-Bribery Officer Procurement Health and Safety Knowledge Management Other (state)
Feedback	A. I confirm that the following issues arose in the last month: (or) B. I confirm that there are no issues to report this month.
Incident details (continue on separate sheet if necessary)	
Action taken to remedy:	
Current position/ further action required:	
Signature:	
COLP signature:	
For COLP: Has the breach register been updated?	

Annex 3G
Record of meetings with complaints partner

Date of meeting:
Attendees:
Agenda: • Review any new complaints/claims received. • Have they been notified to insurers where necessary? • Review existing complaints/claims. Are complaints being handled promptly, fairly and openly? How can they be resolved? • Identify any trends. • Identify any necessary improvements to systems/procedures. • Identify any training needs.
Actions agreed:
Date of next meeting:

4 Reporting to the SRA

Under the SRA Authorisation Rules the firm and/or the COLP is required to provide an annual information report containing such information as may be specified 'in the prescribed form and by the prescribed date' (rule 8.7(a)). The COLP or the firm must also report the following:

- any change in the information provided in an application for authorisation (rule 3.1(b));
- any material non-compliance with the SRA Handbook as soon as reasonably practicable (rule 8.5(c)(ii) and (iii));
- any changes to relevant information about the firm, its employees, managers or interest holders (rule 8.7(c));
- anything which suggests that the firm has, or may have, provided the SRA with information which was or may have been false, misleading, incomplete or inaccurate, or has or may have changed in a material way (rule 8.7(d));
- becoming the sole active partner of a partnership, in the event that they are the sole active partner by reason of the imprisonment, incapacity or the imposition of relevant conditions on, or abandonment of the practice by, the other partner or partners (rule 8.8);
- the loss of the sole remaining solicitor or registered European lawyer (REL) whose role ensured the status of the body as a legal services body (rule 8.9);
- the loss of the sole remaining authorised individual whose role enabled the body to be a licensable body (rule 8.10);
- that the firm ceases to have an approved COLP (rule 18); and
- any unforeseen temporary breach of conditions of a partnership where temporary emergency recognition of a sole practitioner or new firm is required (rules 24 and 25).

The firm is also responsible for making an application for temporary emergency authorisation of a COLP when appropriate (rule 18).

While many of these requirements are placed on the authorised body directly, in most cases it will be the COLP who will take on the role of reporting these issues to the SRA. If the authorised body does not want the COLP to take on some of its reporting responsibilities – for example, it may be more appropriate for HR to report any changes to managers or interest holders – the firm should ensure that the responsibility for such tasks is clearly documented.

4.1 Recording

Records should be kept of all breaches of which the COLP becomes aware. Even in a traditional firm (recognised body/sole practice) where it is no longer necessary to report non-material breaches, it is still a requirement (see rule 8.5(c)(i)(C)) to keep records of all breaches, both non-material as well as material, in order to identify patterns of behaviour which, as a result of the pattern, becomes material. The best way of doing this will depend on the culture, size and structure of the firm. One way might be for employees to complete a breach report form and give it to the COLP (see **Annex 4A**). Another way would be for employees to report breaches orally/by email to the COLP who will then fill in the breach register directly (see **Annex 4B**).

Regardless of the method used to inform the COLP of breaches, the COLP will need to decide how those breaches are recorded and monitored. Ideally, a centralised reporting system providing accurate and up to date data and records of all breaches in compliance should be established. The data should be captured in such a way that patterns of breaches which may be material and thus become reportable can be identified.

We recommend that the COLP reviews the breaches reported on a monthly basis and looks for patterns.

The COLP may also need to consider whether the breach is a 'notifiable circumstance' for insurance purposes. If another person is responsible for claims and complaints, the COLP will need to liaise with that person closely. They will also need to liaise with the COFA.

4.2 The COLP's reporting requirements

The SRA requires reports from the COLP in two circumstances:

1. Material breaches should be reported as soon as reasonably practicable when they arise. The SRA has indicated that as soon as reasonably practicable in most cases means immediately.
2. Rule 8.7 of the SRA Authorisation Rules requires firms to submit an annual information report to the SRA, which, in the case of ABSs, must include details of non-material breaches.

COLPs will be required to report all **material** breaches of compliance, to the SRA. Whilst it used to be the case that all breaches needed reporting at some stage – either immediately or within the annual information report – the SRA's red tape initiative removed the obligation on non-ABS firms to report non-material breaches. In a licensed ABS, there is still the obligation to report all breaches whether material or non-material (the latter within the annual information report).

The SRA's guidance to rule 8 of the SRA Authorisation Rules states:

> The obligations to record non-material breaches under Rule 8.5(c)(i)(C) do not require a record to be kept in any particular form nor do they require the COLP or COFA to make a separate record of each non-material breach of which a record already exists in the firm's papers. How such breaches are recorded and monitored is a matter for firms to decide as part of their compliance plan, bearing in mind that it is necessary for a firm to be able to detect patterns of non-material breaches which, when taken together, amount to material non-compliance which the firm is required to report…

> **Note:** An annual information report has never been issued by the SRA; instead, the SRA uses the practising certificate renewal process to obtain the necessary information.

When deciding if a breach is material, the COLP must consider:

- whether there is a detriment, or risk of a detriment, to the client;
- the extent of the risk of loss of confidence in the practice or in the provision of legal services;
- the scale of the issue; and
- the overall impact on the practice, its clients and third parties.

It is important to note that a series of minor breaches can therefore amount to a material breach under this test. It is for this reason that the COLP should have systems in place to identify patterns of breaches.

Remember also that outcome 10.3 requires a firm to notify the SRA promptly of any material changes including serious financial difficulty, action taken by another regulator and serious failure to comply with or achieve the Principles, rules, outcomes and other requirements of the Handbook. Responsibility for compliance with this outcome lies with all those covered by the Handbook but, in practice, responsibility and accountability for compliance with this outcome will lie with the firm and its managers. The COLP is likely to play an important role in notifying the SRA of such breaches.

There is further guidance and example case studies of what will constitute material breaches on the SRA website (**www.sra.org.uk/solicitors/code-of-conduct/guidance/ case-study/breach-material-non-material-when.page**).

Deciding whether any given situation is a material breach can be difficult; as can balancing the COLP obligations to notify with obligations of the firm to fully investigate and, depending on the circumstances, giving an employee an opportunity to explain their action. In these circumstances, obtaining a second objective opinion from an expert or being a member of a local COLP forum can be useful.

The SRA has stated that if in doubt, you should report.

It will be important for the COLP to ensure that the firm has an open door culture. The COLP will only be able to meet their obligations if fee earners and support staff feel able to report breaches. To aid this, firms should consider having a whistle-blowing policy (see IB(10.10) of the SRA Code of Conduct and **Annex 5A**).

To help give COLPs an idea of scenarios they may come across, a table of common breaches is included (**Table 4.1**). This can be used as a test to gauge what you would do in any given circumstance. We have not provided any definitive answer as to whether they are material breaches because each will turn on their own facts so you will need to go back to basics and apply the criteria set out above. Seek objective advice if necessary.

Whatever decision you make, even if it is that it is not reportable as a material breach, should be documented so you have an audit trail that you can refer to should you be asked to explain your reasoning.

A checklist of action to take in a suspected breach is provided at **Annex 4F.**

Table 4.1 Examples of common breaches

Scenario	SRA Code of Conduct 2011	
	Relevant Principles	Relevant chapters
Failure to comply with court directions	1. uphold the rule of law and the proper administration of justice	Chapter 5
Allowing a client to mislead the court		Chapter 5
Fabrication of evidence by a fee earner	2. act with integrity	Chapter 5
Backdating a document		Chapter 5
Employee Fraud		Chapter 5
Improper/abusive litigation/misleading the court		Chapter 5
Failing to account to a client for commission received as a result of their instructions	3. not allow your independence to be compromised	Chapters 1 and 6
Payment of a prohibited referral fee	4. act in the best interests of each client	Chapter 9
Failure to notify a client of a referral fee		Chapter 9
No client-care letters on any of a fee earner's client files	5. provide a proper standard of service to your clients	Chapter 1
Ignoring a client complaint		Chapter 1
Breach of an undertaking		Chapter 11
Drink driving conviction	6. behave in a way that maintains the trust the public places in you and in the provision of legal services	Chapter 10
Costs order made against client and fee earner pays it out of own pocket and fails to disclose to claims partner.	8. run your business or carry out your role in the business effectively and in accordance with proper governance and sound financial and risk management principles	Chapter 5
Upheld complaint of discrimination by member of staff	9. run your business or carry out your role in the business in a way that encourages equality of opportunity and respect for diversity	Chapter 2
A mortgage statement sent to the wrong client	10. protect client money and assets	Chapter 4
Counsel's advice sent to opposing solicitors in error		Chapter 4
Laptop stolen, not encrypted		Chapter 4
Cyber attack resulting in client information being lost		Chapter 4
Use of client account as a banking facility		Chapter 7

4.3 How to report

The enforcement section of the SRA website contains a 'Report form' which could be used (**www.sra.org.uk/solicitors/enforcement/solicitor-report/other-solicitor-results.page**). Reports can also be made by email (report@sra.org.uk), phone or via the SRA's Red Alert line. A further alternative is to speak to the firm's regulatory manager at the SRA (if appropriate). A draft reporting letter to the SRA can be found at **Annex 4C**.

4.4 Reviewing breaches

Whilst many may view the task of recording and reporting breaches as a 'necessary evil', it is also very worthwhile as part of effective compliance management for the firm. The key is to consider the data which is being compiled and make it useful to the firm as well as to the SRA. We recommend that, on a monthly basis, the breach record is reviewed. If used effectively, the data can identify areas where fee earners and/or support staff require training, show patterns of minor breaches which must be reported as a material breach, and highlight where improvements are needed to current systems and procedures.

Auditing/file reviews should also assist with this process but a common failing is that firms do not have an effective way of maximising the effectiveness of the audit and the data they acquire from it. Dashboard software can assist with this as can a web-based audit procedure.

Annex 4A
Internal breach report form

Date of report:		Client reference:	
Date of breach:		Name of employee reporting (or anonymous):	
Name(s) of employee(s) involved:		Name of department(s) involved:	
Type of breach (if known):			
Brief description of breach:			
Suggested action to remedy:			
Has the client been affected by the breach? If so, how?			
Does the client need to be informed of the breach? [NB consider in conjunction with insurers]			
Has there been a complaint as a result of the breach? If so, please give details.			
Employee signature:			
COLP signature:			
Has the breach register been updated?	Yes/No		

Annex 4B

Breach register

Note: By adopting a key such as the one provided below, the breach register also becomes a useful tool for collecting management information (MI). The MI can then be used to identify areas of weakness in the firm. For example, if the majority of breaches relate to Principle 5 of the SRA Handbook (HP5), it is evident that the firm's staff need further training on client care issues.

	Date of breach	Date breach reported to COLP	Type of breach (see key)	Name of employee/ department	Has the breach been remedied? If so, how?	Was the breach prevent-able?	Is the breach reportable to the SRA now? (Is it a material breach?)	If not, why not?	Date breach reported to the SRA	Current position re. report to SRA
1										
2										
3										
4										
5										
6										
7										
8										
9										
10										

Key	
Type of breach	**Reference**
SRA Handbook Principle X	HP Principle reference
SRA Code of Conduct 2011 outcome (X.X)	CCO(outcome reference)
SRA Accounts Rules 2011	AR
Internal policy	IP
Money Laundering Regulations 2007	MLR
Data Protection Act 1998	DPA
Financial Services Act 2000	FSA
Health and safety regulations	H&S
Undertakings	U

Annex 4C
Draft letter to the SRA reporting a material breach

[Firm's contact details]

Solicitors Regulation Authority
The Cube
199 Wharfside Street
Birmingham
B1 1RN

[Date]

Your ref: *[SRA ref]*
Our ref: *[internal ref]*

Dear Sirs

I write to you in my capacity as COLP, on behalf of my firm, *[name of firm]*, as required under rule 8.5(e) of the SRA Authorisation Rules 2011, to inform you of the following material failure[s] to comply with *[state the principle, outcome or statutory reference]*.

I have deemed the failure to be a material breach on account of [the volume of instances of non-compliance with *[principle, outcome or statutory reference]*/its resulting in detriment or risk of detriment to a client/the scale of the issue/the overall impact it has had on the practice, its clients and third parties].

The history of the breach[es] giving rise to this failure is set out below:

[Provide succinct history covering:

- *timing of breach(es) and discovery;*
- *nature of breach(es);*
- *outcome, principle or statutory requirement breached;*
- *whether breach(es) resulted in any loss or detriment to the client;*
- *cause of breach(es);*
- *status of rectification of error/deficiency in procedures/processes giving rise to breach(es), if applicable;*
- *any recompense given to clients;*
- *any other regulator notified, and*
- *any disciplinary action taken as a result of breach(es) or remedial action to reduce the risk of reoccurrence in the future].*

Should you require any further information in respect of the above matter please do not hesitate to contact me.

Yours faithfully

[Signature of COLP]

[Printed name and position of COLP]

Annex 4D

Breach review form

Date of review:	
Name of reviewer:	
Have there been any breaches reported?	
If so, how many and what are they?	
Is this an increase or decrease from last month?	
Which departments have the breaches occurred in?	
How many breaches in these departments have been reported over the past year?	
Is a specific employee committing a lot of breaches?	
Is any training required?	
Do any new procedures need to be implemented?	
Do any existing policies/ procedures need to be amended?	
Are there any patterns?	
Date of next review:	

Annex 4E

Record of reports submitted to SRA

Note: Examples of results could include: acknowledged and awaiting allocation; under investigation; investigation concluded – no further action; investigation concluded – disciplinary sanction; SDT proceedings.

Breach number / file reference	Date reported	Type of breach	Employee involved	Result
1				
2				
3				
4				
5				
6				

Annex 4F
Checklist of action in a suspected breach

1. Can the breach be immediately rectified? If so, rectify it.
2. If more detailed investigation required, investigate (will take different forms depending upon the circumstances but could include):

   a. Review of specific file
   b. Discussion with fee earner
   c. Discussion with supervising partner
   d. Emergency audit of fee earner's files
   e. Consultation with HR regarding possible disciplinary proceedings

3. Possible suspension of fee earner (in serious circumstances) pending outcome of investigation.
4. Decide if it is a material breach. Take objective independent advice from experts if necessary.
5. If material, report to the SRA – record in register date of report, maintain separate file for the correspondence with the SRA, monitor and fully co-operate with the SRA.
6. Consider also if insurance available in which case notify insurers.
7. Record in breaches register, whether material or not.
8. Review breaches register monthly to ensure kept up to date and trends can be identified.
9. Learn from breach – review systems/procedures that gave rise to the breach and make improvements where necessary.
10. Record steps taken.

5 Additional COLP tools

This chapter contains additional policies, procedures and logs to assist COLPs in the following areas:

- whistle-blowing;
- data protection and information management;
- business continuity;
- complaints handling;
- audit and file review.

Annex 5A
Whistle-blowing policy

Date created:	
Date reviewed:	

1   Policy statement

1.1 We are committed to conducting our business with honesty and integrity, and expect all staff to maintain high standards in accordance with the SRA Handbook. However, we are aware that we face the risk of things going wrong from time to time, or of unknowingly harbouring illegal or unethical conduct. A culture of openness and accountability is essential in order to prevent such situations occurring or to address them when they do occur.

1.2 The aims of this policy are:

(a) to encourage staff to report suspected wrongdoing as soon as possible;
(b) to provide staff with guidance as to how to raise those concerns;
(c) to reassure staff that they are able to raise genuine concerns in good faith without fear of reprisals, even if they turn out to be mistaken.

1.3 This policy does not form part of any employee's contract of employment and it may be amended at any time.

2   Who is covered by this policy?

2.1 This policy applies to any and all individuals working at any and all levels of the firm (collectively referred to as 'staff' in this policy).

3   What is whistle-blowing?

3.1 'Whistle-blowing' is the disclosure of information which relates to suspected wrongdoing or dangers at work. This may include:

(a) criminal activity;
(b) miscarriages of justice;
(c) danger to health and safety;
(d) damage to the environment;
(e) failure to comply with any legal or professional obligations or regulatory requirements, including the SRA Code of Conduct 2011 and SRA Accounts Rules 2011;
(f) bribery;
(g) financial fraud or mismanagement;
(h) negligence;
(i) breach of our internal policies and procedures;

(j)   conduct likely to damage our reputation;

(k)   unauthorised disclosure of confidential information;

(l)   the deliberate concealment of any of the above matters.

3.2 A 'whistle-blower' is a person who raises a genuine concern in good faith relating to any of the above. If you have any genuine concerns related to suspected wrongdoing or danger affecting any of our activities (a 'whistle-blowing concern') you should report it under this policy.

3.3 If you are uncertain whether something is within the scope of this policy you should seek advice from the compliance officer for legal practice (COLP), whose contact details are at the end of this policy.

4   Raising a whistle-blowing concern

4.1 We hope that in many cases you will be able to raise any concerns with your supervisor. You may tell them in person or put the matter in writing if you prefer. They may be able to agree a way of resolving your concern quickly and effectively. In some cases they may refer the matter to the COLP.

4.2 However, where the matter is more serious, or you feel that your supervisor has not addressed your concern, or you prefer not to raise it with them for any reason, please contact the COLP, whose contact details are at the end of this policy.

5   Confidentiality

5.1 We hope that staff will feel able to voice whistle-blowing concerns openly under this policy. However, if you want to raise your concern confidentially, we will make every effort to keep your identity secret. If it is necessary for anyone investigating your concern to know your identity, we will discuss this with you.

5.2 We do not encourage staff to make disclosures anonymously. Proper investigation may be more difficult or impossible if we cannot obtain further information from you. It is also more difficult to establish whether any allegations are credible and have been made in good faith. Whistle-blowers who are concerned about possible reprisals if their identity is revealed should come forward to the COLP and appropriate measures can then be taken to preserve confidentiality.

6   External disclosures

6.1 The aim of this policy is to provide an internal mechanism for reporting, investigating and remedying any wrongdoing in the workplace. In most cases you should not find it necessary to alert anyone externally.

6.2 The law recognises that in some circumstances it may be appropriate for you to report your concerns to an external body such as a regulator. It will very rarely if ever be appropriate to alert the media. We strongly encourage you to seek advice before reporting a concern to anyone external.

6.3 Whistle-blowing concerns usually relate to the conduct of our staff, but they may sometimes relate to the actions of a third party, such as a client, supplier or service provider. The law allows you to raise a concern in good faith with a third party, where you reasonably believe it relates mainly to their actions or something that is legally their responsibility. However, we encourage you to report such concerns internally first. You should contact your supervisor or the COLP for guidance.

7 Investigation and outcome

7.1 Once you have raised a concern, we will carry out an initial assessment to determine the scope of any investigation. We will inform you of the outcome of our assessment. You may be required to attend additional meetings in order to provide further information.

7.2 We will aim to keep you informed of the progress of the investigation and its likely timescale. However, sometimes the need for confidentiality may prevent us giving you specific details of the investigation or any disciplinary action taken as a result. You should treat any information about the investigation as confidential.

7.3 If we conclude that a whistle-blower has made false allegations maliciously, in bad faith or with a view to personal gain, the whistle-blower will be subject to disciplinary action.

8 If you are not satisfied

8.1 While we cannot always guarantee the outcome you are seeking, we will try to deal with your concern fairly and in an appropriate way. By using this policy you can help us to achieve this.

8.2 If you are not happy with the way in which your concern has been handled, you can raise it with one of the [directors/partners/managers] of the firm.

9 Protection and support for whistle-blowers

9.1 Whistle-blowers are sometimes worried about possible repercussions. We aim to encourage openness and will support staff who raise genuine concerns in good faith under this policy, even if they turn out to be mistaken.

9.2 Staff must not suffer any detrimental treatment as a result of raising a concern in good faith. Detrimental treatment includes dismissal, disciplinary action, threats or other unfavourable treatment connected with raising a concern. If you believe that you have suffered any such treatment, you should inform the COLP immediately. If the matter is not remedied you should raise it formally using our grievance procedure.

9.3 Staff must not threaten or retaliate against whistle-blowers in any way. Anyone involved in such conduct will be subject to disciplinary action.

10 Responsibility for the success of this policy

10.1 The [board of directors/partners of the firm/managers of the firm] [has/have] overall responsibility for this policy, and for reviewing the effectiveness of actions taken in response to concerns raised under this policy.

10.2 The COLP has day-to-day operational responsibility for this policy, and must ensure that all managers and other staff who may deal with concerns or investigations under this policy receive regular and appropriate training.

10.3 The COLP, in conjunction with the board, should review this policy from a legal and operational perspective at least once a year.

10.4 All staff are responsible for the success of this policy and should ensure that they use it to disclose any suspected danger or wrongdoing. Staff are invited to comment on this policy and suggest ways in which it might be improved. Comments, suggestions and queries should be addressed to the COLP.

11 Contacts

COLP

[*Name*]

[*Telephone number*]

[*Email address*]

COFA

[*Name*]

[*Telephone number*]

[*Email address*]

[*Managing/senior partner*]

[*Name*]

[*Telephone number*]

[*Email address*]

[*External auditors*]

[*Name*]

[*Telephone number*]

[*Email address*]

Annex 5B
Data protection, confidentiality and information security policy

Purpose

This policy sets out how [*legal practice name*] complies with the Data Protection Act 1998 (DPA), confidentiality issues, information security and the SRA's regulatory requirements including outcome 7.5 and Chapter 4 of the SRA Code of Conduct 2011.

Application

This policy applies to all managers and employees of [*legal practice name*], including those undertaking work through a consultancy arrangement, in a volunteer capacity, on a temporary basis, or through an agency. The term 'employees' is used to refer to managers and employees.

All employees must familiarise themselves, and comply with, this policy and related procedures. Failure to comply with this policy and the related procedures [will/may] result in disciplinary action because of the significant risks of fines, enforcement action, reputational consequences and disciplinary action.

Responsibilities

All employees are responsible for ensuring that all types of data are properly protected. Any issues or concerns about the DPA must be raised with the [DP officer/deputy DP officer/COLP/compliance team].

Relevant legislation

The following legislation must be complied with:

- Data Protection Act 1998 (DPA);
- Computer Misuse Act 1990;
- Regulation of Investigatory Powers Act 2000;
- Telecommunications (Lawful Business Practice) (Interception of Communications) Regulations 2000 (SI 2000/2699);
- Privacy and Electronic Communications (EC Directive) Regulations 2003 (SI 2003/2426);
- SRA Code of Conduct 2011.

Principles

The importance of keeping clients' affairs confidential, protecting personal and sensitive personal data and keeping information secure is fundamental. This policy is designed to cover all these areas so that all employees are clear about their obligations and how to protect data/ensure confidential information is kept confidential.

The DPA establishes a framework of rights and duties designed to protect personal data. The DPA requires that personal data is processed in compliance with the DPA and in accordance with the eight data protection principles. There are specific obligations particularly in relation to an individual's right to access data held about him or her.

Chapter 4 of the SRA Code of Conduct 2011 contains the requirements relating to the duty of confidentiality. While solicitors have a duty to keep clients' affairs confidential, they must also ensure that information belonging to employees, suppliers and third parties is kept confidential. Confidential information can only be released if the individual consents or if that duty is overridden by law, e.g. the money laundering legislation.

The seventh data protection principle requires [*legal practice name*] to have appropriate security to prevent personal data from being accidentally or deliberately compromised.

Employees are reminded that under the Computer Misuse Act 1990, there are three criminal offences:

s.1: Unauthorised access to computer material.
s.2: Unauthorised access with intent to commit or facilitate the commission of further offences.
s.3: Unauthorised modification of computer material.

Employees who are unsure as to whether they are able to access or modify material must contact [the DP officer/deputy DP officer/COLP/compliance officer] for guidance. Any commission of or attempt to commit a criminal offence by an employee will be dealt with in accordance with [*legal practice name*]'s disciplinary policy.

[As [*legal practice name*] monitors [and/or] stores the electronic communications of fee earners and other employees for business/security reasons, [*legal practice name*] must comply with the relevant provisions of the Regulatory and Investigatory Powers Act 2000 and the Telecommunications (Lawful Business Practice) (Interception of Communications) Regulations 2000 (SI 2000/2699). Further information is contained in the [Employee Handbook/the employment policies].]

All employees must keep information about the clients and [*legal practice name*] secure at all times. If an employee is concerned that data or confidential information is at risk, he or she must immediately contact the [DP officer/deputy DP officer/ COLP/compliance team].

Data protection

[*Legal practice name*] must keep certain information on its clients, employees and suppliers to carry out its day-to-day operations, to meet its objectives and to comply with legal obligations. The DPA applies to personal data and sensitive personal data but [*legal practice name*] must keep all client (and employee) information confidential and all information secure.

[*Legal practice name*] is committed to ensuring personal data is dealt with in compliance with the DPA. The aim of the DPA is to protect the rights of individuals (data subjects) about whom [*legal practice name*] holds 'personal data'.

The DPA imposes duties on those who decide how and why such data is processed (data controllers). The definition of 'processing' is obtaining, using, holding, amending, disclosing, destroying or deleting personal data.

[*Legal practice name*] is registered with the Information Commissioner as a data controller. The DP officer is [*name*]. [The deputy DP officer is [*name*].]

'Personal data' means data which relates to a living individual who can be identified from that data or from that data and other information which is in the possession of or likely to come into the possession of [*legal practice name*]. Examples are a person's name, address and date of birth but the definition also includes information which allows an individual to be identified, e.g. a unique reference number. The definition includes any expression of opinion about the individual and any indications of the intentions of the data controller or any other person in respect of the individual.

Personal data includes all data held electronically but also data held in a 'relevant filing system', i.e. non-automated records which are structured in a way which allows ready access to information about individuals.

All personal data must be processed in accordance with the eight data protection principles which require that data will:

- be obtained fairly and lawfully and not be processed unless certain conditions are met;
- be obtained for a specific and lawful purpose;
- be adequate, relevant but not excessive;
- be accurate and kept up to date;
- not be held longer than necessary;
- be processed in accordance with the rights of data subjects;
- be subject to appropriate security measures;
- not be transferred outside the European Economic Area (EEA).

[*Legal practice name*] must process personal data in accordance with one of the conditions for processing (usually consent) and fairly and lawfully.

Clients are provided with the necessary information about how their data will be processed in the client care letter/terms of business. If clients have any queries, employees must contact the [DP officer/deputy DP officer/COLP/compliance team] for advice.

Sensitive personal data

[*Legal practice name*] processes data about clients which will include sensitive personal data. The terms of business explain to clients how their data will be processed and seek explicit consent to the processing. If a client has a query about sensitive personal data, guidance should be sought from the [DP officer/deputy DP officer/COLP/compliance team].

All employees must ensure that they recognise sensitive personal data. All employees must ensure that, wherever the data is held, i.e. on computer or in a relevant filing system (or a paper file), it is properly protected and held securely.

Sensitive personal data is personal data about:

(a) racial or ethnic origin;
(b) political opinions;
(c) religious or other beliefs of a similar nature;
(d) trade union membership;
(e) physical or mental health or condition;
(f) sexual life;
(g) the commission or alleged commission of any offence;
(h) any proceedings for any offence committed or alleged to have been committed, the disposal of such proceedings or the sentence of any court in such proceedings.

All employees will be trained on data protection issues and must attend the data protection training so that they understand what is meant by personal data and sensitive personal data and what their obligations are.

Employees

[*Legal practice name*] also processes data about prospective and current employees in accordance with [*legal practice name*]'s HR policies and the employment legislation as follows:

• Information on applicants for posts, including references.
• Employee information – contact details, bank account number, payroll information, supervision and appraisal notes.

All employees must comply with the same obligations in relation to employee data as they do in relation to client data.

Duty of confidentiality

The duty of confidentiality to clients is a fundamental duty and for solicitors and their employees. Outcome 4.1 of the SRA Code of Conduct 2011 requires that the affairs of clients are kept confidential unless disclosure is required or permitted by law or the client consents.

Employees must tell a client all the information relevant to that retainer of which he or she has personal knowledge under outcome 4.2. Where the duty of confidentiality to one client conflicts with the duty of disclosure to another client, the duty of confidentiality takes precedence under outcome 4.3. Employees must ensure that they comply with [legal practice name]'s conflicts policy.

Employees must comply with outcome 4.4 and must not act for client A in a matter where A has an interest adverse to client B and B is a client for whom confidential information is held which is material to A in that matter. The only exception to that prohibition is where a legal practice is able to use an information barrier. [Legal practice name] [does/does not] use information barriers [as permitted by the relevant procedure].

[Legal practice name] has effective systems and controls which are set out in the policies and procedures to identify risks to client confidentiality and to mitigate those risks, as required by outcome 4.5. Employees must comply with [legal practice name]'s policies and procedures.

Employees must ensure conversations about client matters, which take place outside a secure environment, e.g. in the reception area, the lift and outside the office (especially with mobile phone conversations in public places, including trains), cannot be overheard.

Employees must not name clients or inform or confirm to a third party that [legal practice name] acts for someone unless that client has expressly given consent. This extends to enquiries from law enforcement as to whether [legal practice name] is acting for a particular individual which must be dealt with in accordance with the policy on responding to requests from law enforcement.

Employees must not answer any questions from the press or even confirm that [legal practice name] is acting for a particular client. Employees cannot provide an address (but can offer to pass on a letter to a client) and must refer all enquiries to the [DP officer/deputy DP officer/compliance team] or the supervising partner.

When in court, employees must ensure that they do not discuss the client's matter in the hearing of the press or third parties, including the other parties to the case unless it is in the course of carrying out the client's instructions.

All employees must be aware of their duties under this policy and keep clients' affairs confidential except in the following situations:

- the client consents or asks that confidential information be provided;
- confidential information has to be provided by law.

All employees must comply with this policy and related procedures, attend training provided, raise any queries with the [DP officer/deputy DP officer/COLP/compliance team] and report any breaches or allegations or suspicions of breaches of confidentiality to the [DP officer/deputy DP officer/COLP/compliance team].

While the above provisions relate to clients, employees must ensure that they also keep information about other employees, third parties and suppliers confidential, as required by the law of confidence. The provisions apply equally to other employees, third parties and suppliers.

Personal conflicts

If employees have any personal knowledge of or any close connection to the client or others involved in any matter on which they are working, they must comply with [*legal practice name*]'s conflicts policy.

Information security

All files, laptops, smartphones and mobile phones must be kept with the employee at all times to minimise the risk of breaches of confidentiality and ensure that information is kept securely.

All electronic devices issued by the legal practice will be encrypted so that the risk of data loss is reduced. Employees must comply with [*legal practice name*]'s policy in relation to any confidential information which may be held on their personal devices.

Employees are not permitted to use USB sticks, or other mechanisms of transferring data, on electronic devices owned by [*legal practice name*] unless approval has been received from the [DP officer/deputy DP officer/IT/COLP].

When out of the office, files/papers must not be carried in a way which shows information that can identify the client (e.g. Mrs McGregor, 43 Acacia Avenue, Divorce). Files/papers must not be left in unlocked cars, and in no circumstances in cars overnight. If it is unavoidable, e.g. due to another appointment or court hearing, files/papers [may/must] be kept in the boot of a locked car.

All waste/unwanted letters and documents (including drafts and unwanted photocopies) must be disposed of securely [in the confidential waste/*other*].

Employees must not:

- install any software without authorisation;
- disclose their password to anyone else;
- use other people's log-in details;
- take equipment, data, information sources or software offsite unless they have written authority to do so;
- copy files from the network server into a personal directory without authority.

Employees must:

- log off when leaving their PC or workstation unattended;
- change their password, if it appears to have been found out/in accordance with [*legal practice name*]'s policy;
- ensure that no member of the public has access to the computer system;
- always ensure laptops and mobile devices are secured in unattended offices;
- ensure data is transferred between laptops/mobile devices and the main system as soon as possible to preserve its integrity and in accordance with [*legal practice name*]'s policy;
- keep master copies of important data on the network server and not on a PC's local C drive or USB sticks. Data will not be backed up unless it is on the network server and so it is at risk;
- ask for advice from [IT/DP officer/deputy DP officer], if it is necessary to store, transmit or handle large quantities of data, e.g. DVDs or images.

If there is any loss of data or risk of loss, employees must immediately contact the [DP officer/deputy DP officer/COLP/compliance team] who will advise what to do next.

Subject access requests (SARs)

The DPA gives individuals the right to access personal data held about them on computer and in relevant filing systems. Any person wishing to exercise this right should apply in writing to the [DP officer/deputy officer/COLP/compliance team]. The terms of business provide details of how to make a SAR.

If a request is made quoting the DPA or if an individual makes a subject access request, that must be referred to the [DP officer/deputy officer/COLP/compliance team] immediately. Clients may also ask for details of information held about them without mentioning the word 'data' or the data protection legislation; all such requests must be forwarded immediately to the [DP officer/deputy officer/COLP/ compliance team] as that request may still be a SAR.

There are strict timescales for compliance with a SAR and failure to comply can result in a significant fine from the ICO. Employees must comply with [*legal practice name*]'s procedure for dealing with SARs.

Accuracy of data

Employees must ensure that data is as accurate as possible; if data is or appears to be inaccurate, misleading or not up to date, employees must take reasonable steps to amend/update the information as soon as possible. Data only needs to be kept up to date where necessary and employees should seek guidance if they are not sure whether the data needs to be updated. Clients have the right to prevent processing of their personal data in some circumstances and the right to correct, rectify, block or erase information regarded as wrong. Any concerns must be discussed with the [DP officer/deputy DP officer/COLP/compliance team].

Retention and destruction of data

Personal data must be retained or disposed of securely in accordance with [*legal practice name*]'s data retention and destruction policy.

Data controllers/processors

Personal data must not be disclosed to another party unless they are a data controller or a data processor (as defined by this policy), or it is for the purposes of the case. The client must always be advised to whom the data will be disclosed and why.

Before sending data to a data controller or a data processor, the employee must ensure that proper contractual arrangements are in place to protect the data. Alternatively, the employee must contact the [DP officer/deputy DP officer/COLP/ compliance team] to determine whether there is already a contractual arrangement or what further steps need to be taken. [*Legal practice name*] must ensure that the data controller or data processor is clear as to the basis on which they will hold the data, when they will return it, what the security arrangements are and what will happen if there is any data loss.

The [DP officer/deputy DP officer/COLP/compliance team] is responsible for ensuring that appropriate due diligence is undertaken and that [*legal practice name*] is registered with the ICO. The [DP officer/deputy DP officer/COLP/compliance team] will record the details of the data controller or data processor on the data controller/data processor log. If an employee has any queries about the way in which a data controller or data processor is dealing with data, he or she must contact the [DP officer/deputy DP officer/COLP/compliance team].

Breaches of policy

Breaches of this policy may require disclosure to the SRA, which may result in disciplinary action, given the obligations under Chapter 10 of the SRA Code of Conduct 2011. A report may also need to be made to the ICO under [*legal practice name*]'s policy on reporting to the ICO.

Further advice

If there are concerns regarding a client or a retainer and potential breaches of confidentiality, employees must contact the [DP officer/deputy DP officer/COLP/ compliance team] immediately for advice.

Definitions

Personal data – data which relates to a living individual who can be identified from that data, or from that data and other information which is in the possession of, or is likely to come into the possession of, the data controller, and includes any expression of opinion about the individual and any indication of the intentions of the data controller or any other person in respect of the individual.

Data subject means a living individual who is the subject of personal data.

Data controller means a person (usually an organisation) who (alone or jointly or in common with other persons) determines the purposes for which and the manner in which any personal data is, or is to be, processed. However, two or more persons (usually organisations) can be joint data controllers where they act together to decide the purpose and manner of any data processing. The term 'in common' applies where two or more persons share a pool of personal data that they process independently of each other.

Data processor – in relation to personal data, means any person (other than an employee of the data controller) who processes the data on behalf of the data controller.

Related policies and procedures

The following policies and procedures must be considered when complying with this policy:

- Disciplinary policy
- Subject access request procedure
- Responding to requests from third parties policy
- Reporting to the ICO policy
- Data retention and destruction procedure
- Ongoing monitoring procedure
- Social media policy
- Data loss policy
- DPA complaints policy
- Training procedure.

Glossary

COLP	compliance officer for legal practice
DPA	Data Protection Act 1998
DP officer	data protection officer
ICO	Information Commissioner's Office
SAR	subject access request
SRA	Solicitors Regulation Authority

Date of effect/date of review

This policy shall come into effect on [*date*] and will be reviewed annually.

Annex 5C
Information management policy

Policy statement

The practice recognises the importance of ensuring the safety and security of the information that it holds in electronic and hard/documentary form. This policy contains details of the practice's approach to the subject of information management, and contains procedures and principles that are to be followed by everyone in the practice.

Any breaches of this policy could have far reaching and serious consequences for the practice, and it is essential that it is complied with at all times. Breaches of the policy will be treated as extremely serious by the practice, and could result in disciplinary proceedings.

Scope

This policy covers information created, and assets held, by the practice.

This policy applies to all individuals working at every level and grade, including partners, senior managers, officers, directors, employees, consultants, contractors, trainees, home workers, part-time and fixed-term employees, casual and agency staff and volunteers, collectively referred to as staff in this policy.

Third parties who have access to the practice's electronic communication systems and equipment are also required to comply with this policy.

Purpose

The policy is intended to eliminate mismanagement of data wherever possible, in order to avoid or mitigate some or all of the following consequences (the list is not exhaustive):

- proceedings under the Data Protection Act 1998;
- the inability to offer services;
- reputational and/or financial damage;
- proceedings for negligence;
- breaches of confidentiality;
- breaches of the SRA Code of Conduct 2011 and any other legislative or regulatory requirements.

Categories of information assets

The practice holds electronic and hard copy (mainly paper) information assets, as detailed below (the list is not exhaustive).

1.   Hard/document-based information assets

- Practice documents (leases, standard forms, minutes, etc.).
- Client documents (letters, agreements, court orders, bill of costs, etc.).
- HR staff documents (contracts, holiday and sickness records, etc.).
- Precedents (departmental paragraphs, etc.).
- Marketing customer relationship management (CRM) (contact information, event acceptance, etc.).
- Templates and forms (departmental).
- Financial (practice reports, analysis spreadsheets, etc.).

2.   Electronic information assets

The electronic information assets are described in the table below, together with descriptions of how they, and 'hard' information assets, are retained and stored by the practice.

[*Each practice will need to make amendments that represent their assets and individual approaches and responsibilities for those assets within the table. The information presently in the table is an example of one practice's approach.*]

Asset description	Media type	Format type	Backup type	Lead responsibility
'Hard' assets as described above	Paper	Within cabinet drawers and paper folders/lever arch folders	Archiving house and business continuity planning	Fee earners and practice manager

Identified risks associated with the data held

The following table outlines the potential risks associated with the data assets identified above, together with measures that the practice takes to prevent, minimise or mitigate those risks. References to BCP mean the business continuity plan, and DRP mean the disaster recovery plan.

Risk description	First line	Second line
Fire/flood/major incident	• Key documents retained in metal cabinets and fireproof safe/cupboard • 'Hard' assets retained in cabinets and shelves above floor level • Key documents scanned for electronic storage	Annual risk assessment with operational BCP and DRP
Virus attacks	Practice wide antivirus software. Training and awareness training on regulations, operational procedures and policies	Full backups of data on internal and external data storage solutions
Damaging integrity of data through lack of knowledge or malice	Training and awareness training on regulations, operational procedures and policies	Full backups of data on internal and external data storage solutions
Password sharing	Training and awareness training on regulations, operational procedures and policies	Reinforcement of security requirements at team meetings
Remote connection	Full SSL (Secure Sockets Layer) VPN connections for all external connecting devices (including laptops, PDAs)	
External attack	Full firewall protection	Full backups of data on internal and external data storage solutions

Management roles and responsibilities

Responsibility for the management of electronic data lies with [name], and the responsibility for hard information assets lies with:

• fee earners in the case of such assets relevant to the matter files; and
• [name] for all other such assets.

The responsibilities include (the list is not exhaustive):

• management and security of the data;
• ensuring that the data conforms to all policies relating to its use, retention and storage;
• ensuring that company records are created, maintained and archived in accordance with the relevant policies;
• management of all records;
• management of risks to the data;
• ensuring that sufficient resources are devoted to these tasks.

Training

Training on information management forms part of the induction process for new partners, fee earners and members of staff. Additionally, it is included in the list of 'generic' training that applies to all members of the practice, and which will be delivered as indicated in the practice's training plan at intervals not exceeding [*frequency with which this training will be provided*].

At the discretion of managers and team leaders, training can also be presented at ad hoc intervals during team/departmental meetings.

Information management principles and guidance

The practice's management and use of information assets will comply with the seven information management principles given below.

1. Information is a corporate resource which belongs to the practice and its clients.

As a consequence, information must be:

Available

2. Staff will only limit colleagues' access to information that they create or capture if its sensitivity requires it.
3. Information will be managed consistently, including by the use of approved naming conventions and filing structures.

Appropriate

4. Everyone will ensure that information is accurate and fit for purpose.
5. Information will be retained and disposed of appropriately.
6. Everyone is personally responsible for the effective management of the information that they create, capture or use.
7. In managing information, everyone will comply with the relevant statutory and regulatory requirements – including the requirement not to destroy information where there is a legal obligation to retain it.

Information security

A common sense approach must be taken to information security. Individuals are responsible for the security of information that they create or store. Particular care should be exercised with information that may be commercially sensitive (e.g. relating to project plans or bid tenders). When dealing with paper documents, this includes locking filing cabinets and, when dealing with electronic data, the facility to change folder and file user access rights.

Storage and retrieval of information

A consistent approach is important to preserve the quality and integrity of information, and to ensure that it can be readily identified and retrieved.

Staff should consider the retrieval needs of others within the practice when storing information. For example, this could require the use of document titles, and the addition of relevant keywords in order to enable others to retrieve the document. This is particularly important with regard to emails.

Documents should be placed within the practice's network storage facilities at the earliest opportunity, in order to help prevent information from becoming outdated before others, who may have an interest in it, can gain access.

Dissemination of information

Anyone who receives information which is not relevant to them must pass it to an appropriate individual within the practice who can determine whether it should be retained.

There will be times when consideration should be given as to whether information should be published on the practice's intranet, and this may mean seeking advice from [*name*].

Retention and disposal of information

Information that is inaccurate or out of date should not be kept (unless it has a historical value). Indeed, keeping inaccurate information can be damaging. Information that is no longer required for business purposes, or in order to comply with a legal obligation, should be deleted or destroyed.

Certain information, including matter files, is retained as indicated in [*location of where file retention periods are indicated*].

Intellectual property of others (copyright)

A document will not incorporate the intellectual property of others unless the practice has the relevant rights. Documents (including scanning) must not be entered into the information system unless the practice owns or has obtained the copyright to do so. Material specifically addressed to the practice can be entered into the information management system.

Data Protection Act 1998

Everyone is responsible for complying with the eight principles relating to personal information (summarised below) that are contained in the Data Protection Act 1998.

Such information must:

1. be fairly and lawfully processed;
2. be processed for specified purposes;
3. be adequate, relevant and not excessive;
4. be accurate and, where necessary, kept up to date;
5. not be kept for longer than is necessary;
6. be processed in line with the rights of the individual;
7. be kept secure; and
8. not be transferred to countries outside the European Economic Area unless the information is adequately protected.

Policy review

[*Name*] will conduct a documented review of this policy at least annually to ensure that it is current, and in effective use throughout the practice.

Relevant definitions

Document

A 'document' can be defined as information that is stored as a single entity on some medium, e.g. on a computer drive or paper file, etc.

The term also covers information in what might seem non-documentary formats, e.g. computer applications and databases.

Record

A 'record' can be defined as a document which has content, context and structure, and which provides evidence of a business transaction, or contains information needed to carry on the practice's business.

A record can either be created within or without the practice. It may be created to fulfil a legal requirement, and may be required as evidence or to satisfy accountability.

Records are derived from documents, therefore all records will be documents, but not all documents will be records. For example, a publication in a library provides information, and is therefore a document, but it is not a record because it does not provide evidence of an activity.

Annex 5D
Data loss policy

Purpose

This policy sets out how [*legal practice name*] complies with the data protection legislation, confidentiality issues, information security and the SRA's regulatory requirements including outcome 7.5 and Chapter 4 of the SRA Code of Conduct 2011, in the event of a loss of personal data.

Application

This policy applies to all managers and employees of [*legal practice name*], including those undertaking work through a consultancy arrangement, in a volunteer capacity, on a temporary basis, or through an agency. The term 'employees' is used to refer to managers and employees.

All employees must familiarise themselves and comply with this policy. Failure to comply with this policy [will/may] result in disciplinary action because of the significant risks of fines, enforcement action, reputational consequences and disciplinary action.

Seventh principle of the Data Protection Act 1998

Data controllers must take appropriate technical and organisational measures against unauthorised or unlawful processing of personal data and against accidental loss or destruction of, or damage to, personal data. Failure to do so can result in fines of up to £500,000 from the ICO.

Responsibilities

All employees are responsible for ensuring that all types of data are properly protected and kept secure.

Data security breach or potential loss of personal data

If any employee becomes aware of any:

- loss or potential loss of personal data;
- breach or potential breach of confidentiality;
- loss of laptop or other device, e.g. smartphone or mobile phone (whether it belongs to [*legal practice name*] or to an employee personally) which may result in a loss of data or breach of confidentiality;
- breach of information security, whether physical or electronic;

the employee must immediately inform the [DP officer/deputy DP officer/COLP/ compliance team/supervising partner] so that appropriate action can be taken and because serious breaches must be reported to the ICO/SRA.

To enable the [DP officer/deputy DP officer/COLP/compliance team] to determine whether the breach is serious, the employee must provide the information [requested/set out in the data loss reporting form].

On receipt of the report, the [DP officer/deputy DP officer/COLP/compliance team] will respond to the incident.

Stage 1 – containment and recovery phase

The [DP officer/deputy DP officer/COLP/compliance team] will:

- investigate the breach [and] in conjunction with the COLP and the managing partner, [and] ensure they have appropriate resources;
- establish who needs to be made aware of the breach and inform them of what they must do to assist in the containment exercise;
- establish whether anything can be done to recover any lost data/limit the damage the breach [may/can] cause;
- identify any third party involved in the breach and liaise with them, as appropriate;
- where appropriate, inform the police and the ICO/SRA.

Stage 2 – assessing the risks phase

The [DP officer/deputy DP officer/COLP/compliance team] will assess the risks which may be associated with the breach before taking any steps after the immediate containment, as follows:

- What type of data is involved?
- How sensitive is the data?
- If the data has been lost or stolen, is there any protection, e.g. encryption?
- What has happened to the data?
- How could the data be misused?
- How many individuals are affected?
- Who are the individuals affected?
- What harm can come to those individuals as a result of the loss/breach?
- Are there wider consequences to consider?
- If an individual's bank details have been lost, what steps can be taken to prevent fraud?

The [DP officer/deputy DP officer/COLP/compliance team] will also consider:

- What are the potential adverse consequences for individuals?
- How serious/substantial are they?
- How likely is it that they will happen?

Depending on the conclusion, the [DP officer/deputy DP officer/COLP/compliance team] will decide who needs to be notified.

Stage 3 – notification of breaches phase

The [DP officer/deputy DP officer/COLP/compliance team] will consider the following in determining whether (and whom) to notify:

- [*Legal practice notice*]'s legal/contractual requirements.
- Will notification help to meet the security obligation in relation to the seventh data protection principle?
- Can notification help the individual?
- If a large number of people are affected or there are serious consequences, the ICO should be informed.
- How notification can be made appropriate for particular groups of individuals, e.g. vulnerable adults.
- The dangers of over-notifying.

The [DP officer/deputy DP officer/COLP/compliance team] will consider the following before deciding who to notify, what information to provide and how the information/message is to be communicated:

Who

- SRA (material or systemic breaches).
- ICO (significant breach/volume/sensitivity of data).
- Client/joint data controller/data processor/third party/insurers/banks.

How

- How to notify.
- How individuals can obtain further information.

What

- What information to notify.
- What steps have been taken to respond to the risks.
- What steps can be taken by, e.g. individuals to protect themselves.

If a decision is made to notify the ICO, the [DP officer/deputy DP officer/COLP] will report to the ICO in accordance with [*legal practice name*]'s procedure.

If the [DP officer/deputy DP officer] decides that there is a material or systemic breach, all relevant information will be passed to the COLP to decide whether to report to the SRA.

If the [DP officer/deputy DP officer/compliance team] decides that the client should be advised, [all relevant information will be shared with the COLP/the COLP will be advised of the circumstances] and the [COLP/DP officer] will decide how to advise the client and what information to provide.

If the [DP officer/deputy DP officer/compliance team] decides that a third party/bank should be advised, [all relevant information will be shared with the COLP/the COLP will be advised of the circumstances] and the [COLP/DP officer] will decide what information to provide and what assistance to seek.

Any decision to report to the insurers (and what information to provide) will be taken by the COLP, in conjunction with the [DP officer/deputy DP officer/managing partner].

Stage 4 – Evaluation and response phase

The [DP officer/deputy DP officer] will evaluate the effectiveness of [*legal practice name*]'s response to the breach by considering the following:

- What was the cause of the breach/reason for the loss?
- What steps can be taken to prevent a recurrence?
- Was the response hampered by inadequate policies or a lack of a clear allocation of responsibility?
- Could existing procedures lead to another breach?
- Where can improvements be made to the systems and controls?

The [DP officer/deputy DP officer/compliance team] should ensure they:

- know what personal data is held, where and how it is stored;
- establish where the major risks are and why, how much sensitive personal data is held, and whether data is stored across the business or concentrated in one location;
- consider the risks involved in sharing data with or disclosing data to others, whether the method of transmission is secure, whether the minimum amount of data is being shared/disclosed, which data controllers/data processors/third parties the practice shares with and whether the contracts need to be amended/improved;
- identify weak points in the existing security measures such as the use of portable storage devices;
- monitor employees' awareness of security issues and address any gaps through training or tailored advice;
- consider whether to establish a group of fee earners/support staff to discuss 'what if' scenarios to highlight risks and weaknesses and provide an opportunity for employees to suggest solutions;
- implement and test a business continuity plan for data security breaches;
- identify a group of people responsible for reacting to reports of breaches of security or significant data loss.

Related policy

Data protection policy and related policies and procedures

Glossary

COLP	compliance officer for legal practice
DP officer	data protection officer
ICO	Information Commissioner's Office
SRA	Solicitors Regulation Authority

Date of effect/date of review

This policy shall come into effect on [*date*]. This policy shall be reviewed annually.

Annex 5E

Data loss reporting form

Fee earner/ department	Name of client(s)	What was lost?	Personal or sensitive personal data	How was it lost?	When was it lost?	Likely impact	How was the loss discovered?	Where is the data now?	To whom has the loss been reported?	Lessons learnt

Annex 5F

Business continuity plan

[*Name of firm*]

Crisis Management Team leader: [*name*]

Deputy: [*name*]

Location: [*location*]

Date: [*date*]

Issue: [*version*]

> **Important:** This document contains staff contact information and should be used for business continuity purposes only. It is the personal responsibility of all plan holders to secure their respective copies to ensure the confidentiality of the information within.

SECTION 1: Introduction

Version control and review

The internal and external contacts directory at [*practice name*] is to be reviewed on a [*insert details, e.g. quarterly basis*]; the remainder of this document is to be reviewed annually or as may be required in the light of changing business circumstances and events.

Document history

Version no.	Date	Authors	Description of change
1.0			New plan
2.0			Full review – new plan

Distribution/storage

Action: 2 copies: hard copy (office); soft copy on USB (home)	Information
All CMT members	CMT Battle Box (x 3)

SECTION 2: Business continuity plan

Business continuity policy essentials

All Crisis Management Team (CMT) members must be familiar with the practice's business continuity policy essentials set out below. Plan users should refer to this page during an incident.

Purpose

To provide our clients with the highest service levels of any law firm.

Business continuity strategy

[To minimise the interruption to normal levels of operational functionality and service to all the firm's stakeholders, operational partners and staff.]

or

[To maintain our client services with minimal interruption so as to continue to provide the highest service levels of any law firm.]

Scope

The scope of [*name of firm*]'s business continuity management system includes [*specify departments*] and all the firm's staff.

It also includes embedded contractors and partners who may be critical to its recovery.

Strategic recovery objectives

- To ensure the safety and welfare of the firm's staff, contractors, visitors and the public.
- To restore facilities at affected site(s) [*insert location(s)*].
- To restore IT at affected site(s).
- To resume fee-earning operations as quickly as possible.
- To provide services and facilities to operational partners and stakeholders.

These strategic recovery objectives are supported by department-level business continuity strategies within the Facilities, Media, IT, HR, Company Finance and Business Continuity CMT.

Planning assumptions

- A threat or an incident could be internal or external and could affect the sites at [*insert locations*] or impact on an area-wide scale (local, regional or national).
- A site could be lost (destroyed) totally by any of a number of causes.
- Access could be denied to a site for up to [*x*] months; one or both sites may suffer from the same event and be similarly affected.
- [*x*]% of people in the firm's premises could be casualties and [*x*]% of these casualties could become fatalities. 'People' includes staff, contractors, visitors and the public.
- Significant disruption to IT may occur.
- The only conceivable threat to the firm as a whole is either a severe pandemic or a catastrophic IT failure.

Pandemic planning

- The firm recognises the inevitability of a pandemic occurring at some time.
- A comprehensive pandemic annex to the main plan will be maintained.
- It will be based on best practice guidance and the most up-to-date advice on infection rates and mortality as published by the UK Health Protection Agency, the UK Department of Health and the World Health Organization.

Methodology

The firm has adopted the UK's 'Gold (strategic level), Silver (tactical level) and Bronze (operational response level)' system (as recommended in current Home Office advice literature) as a model on which to base management response to serious incidents. The system as applied to the firm is outlined below:

Gold Strategic Control Group (SCG) comprises:

Name	Appointment	Crisis role

Role

- To determine strategy in an incident.
- To prioritise issues affecting the firm as a whole.
- To give directions to 'Silver teams' at office locations for action.
- To deal with any press or media inquiries.

Silver Incident Management Team (IMT) comprises:

Name	Appointment	Crisis role

Role

- To apply strategic direction in the local context.
- To issue local direction and tasking to operational response groups.
- To report progress and issues to the SCG.

Note: Two IMTs could be active in the case of mutual support requirements being invoked between [*specify*] and [*specify*]. The IMT at the unaffected site will probably not be in permanent session and will be acting in support of the affected site.

Bronze Operational Response Teams (ORTs)

The composition of ORTs will vary depending on the nature of the incident. ORTs will work to the direction of their representative in the Silver IMT. Some ORTs may also report back on progress to the SCG, e.g. IT ORTs, but will always take local instruction.

Business continuity responsibilities

- [*Name*], [*job title*], is the Management Board sponsor for business continuity.
- [*Name*], [*job title*], is responsible for the implementation, operation and maintenance of business continuity.
- Every member of staff should be aware of the firm's business continuity policy and have a good understanding of their department's business continuity plan.

Crisis management structure

The firm's crisis management structure (below) is to operate in event of a major incident:

[*insert diagram*]

Crisis Management Team: roles and responsibilities

Name	Role	CMT function	Responsibilities

SECTION 3. Crisis Management Team leader

Overview of team plan

Purpose

The purpose of the CMT leader at the firm is to lead and manage response to an incident that seriously interferes with the operational functionality and service. This will minimise disruption and enable the practice to resume normal levels of service and business activity as quickly and as smoothly as possible.

Phases/milestones

The business continuity plan (BCP) is to be delivered in four phases with key milestones monitored and reported up through the chain of command (department to CMT to Managing Partner/Head of Legal):

Phase	Milestones
Phase 1: Incident response	Building confirmed clear of all staff and visitors
	Invocation decision
	Staff instructed to move to alternative site
Phase 2: Action at recovery site	IT systems functional
	Status report on affected site
Phase 3: Action at business as usual (BAU) site	
Phase 4: Post-incident follow-up	

Phases are illustrated in the plans as follows:

Incident response	Action at recovery site	Recover to BAU site	Post-incident follow-up

Invocation of BCP

- **Authority:** [*e.g.* Managing Partner/Head of Legal]
- **Method:** Initiated by CMT Chair or, in his absence, CMT Deputy Chair by a directive communicated by means of [telephone calls/*other*] cascaded to and then down through departments and teams.
- **Telephone/cascade:** Initiated by CMT Chair or Deputy Chair; cascade is at [*insert details*].

Supporting strategies for reference

Media team

The practice's Media team supporting strategy to the overarching crisis strategy is to:

- maintain the reputation of [*practice name*] by [*insert brief details*].

HR team

The firm's HR team supporting strategy to the overarching crisis strategy is to:

- provide appropriate support and assistance to [*insert brief details*].

Facilities Management department

The firm's Facilities Management department supporting strategy to the overarching crisis strategy is to:

- make available to staff, at all times, adequate premises and business infrastructure as to: [*insert brief details*]
  - document and buildings recovery;
  - insurance policies;
  - disaster recovery (DR) sites and mutual aid.

IT team

The strategy of the IT team in crisis will be to:

- recover the IT systems in a progressive fashion [*insert details*].

Finance team

The firm's Finance team supporting strategy to the overarching crisis strategy is to:

- ensure the financial stability of the firm during and following any incident by [*insert details*].

Critical locations

Primary location

(a) Management Board – emergency management room: [*designate room/venue*].
(b) CMT incident control centre: [*designate CMT room/venue*].

Secondary location

(a) Management Board – emergency management room: [*designate room/venue*].
(b) CMT incident control centre: [*designate room/venue*].

The firm's alternative command and control centre:

[*Insert maps as appropriate*]

PHASE 1
CMT leader incident response

Incident response	Action at recovery site	Recover to BAU site	Post-incident follow-up

Objective

Lead the management of the firm's response to an incident so that the Management Board, groups and departments understand what has happened and respond correctly.

- Target completion time: 2 hours

Tasks

Incident response tasks	Instruction
Target completion time: 2 hours	
Obtain any casualty update	Report any casualties to executive and HR for action
Alert recovery site providers and activate BCP	Tel [*insert number*] and give instructions Inform all departmental heads that plan is active
Convene initial meeting and confirm times for move to DR site	
Obtain initial facilities report on site and review any timings	
Additional time: 2 hours	
Initiate update reports for clients	Liaise with Media team and gain approval from managing partner
Consider local press release if required	As above

PHASE 2
CMT leader action at recovery site

Incident response	Action at recovery site	Recover to BAU site	Post-incident follow-up

Objective

Lead the management of the recovery of the practice's normal business activities so as to resume normal services and operations after a disruption and possible dislocation as quickly as possible.

- Target completion time: [*number of hours*]

Tasks

Incident response tasks	Instruction
Target completion time: 2–8 hours	
Review systems capabilities	With IT representative, report status to executive *Note*: what is *not* operational is most important as it can reduce capability
Make adjustments to accommodation requirements based on matters and their criticality	Inform all legal departments as to outcomes
Confirm all remote access systems are functioning	
Target completion time: 8 hours and onwards	

PHASE 3
Recover to business as usual site

Incident response	Action at recovery site	Recover to BAU site	Post-incident follow-up

Objective

Lead the management of the recovery of all the practice's business activities and staff from temporary recovery sites to original workplaces or medium-/long-term alternative sites so as to resume BAU after a disruption/dislocation.

- Target completion time: [*number of hours*]

Tasks

Tasks	Instruction
Obtain site report from FM and make an appreciation of re-occupancy	
Obtain any amendments to seating and or locations that might be required by staff departmental heads	

PHASE 4
Post-incident follow-up action

Incident response	Action at recovery site	Recover to BAU site	Post-incident follow-up

Objective

Review the cause of the disruption/dislocation, the incident response, occupation and set-up of recovery workplaces, the operation of all fee-earning and support activities and the re-occupation and resumption of functions at the original site. This will help assess performance, learn lessons and ensure that individual staff needs have been and are continuing to be met.

Tasks

Tasks	Instruction
Initiate internal inquiry	Determine inquiry leader, duration, terms of reference and report format

Annex 5G
Business continuity risk matrix

Disruption	Duration of loss	Risk rating	Financial loss	Client impact	Damage to reputation	Regulatory issues	Steps to minimise risk	Recovery time objective	Recovery point objective
Small contained fire in the main office building	One day	Significant	Two hours' loss for the department	Loss of communication to department for [x] hours	Small, if communication is contained	Limited	Fire drill practice every six months Two back-up computers in store Communication to department heads by mobiles using telephone cascade during evacuation	Two hours	All fee earners back in work stations
Large fire in main office building rendering it unusable for several weeks	Six weeks	Very severe	Substantial (refer to insurance cover)	Possibly very severe if unable to operate from an alternative site within a few hours	Possibly very severe if unable to operate from an alternative site within a few hours	Need to ensure an alternative site is available	Senior management to meet to decide on a plan for continuing business Communication to department heads by mobiles using telephone cascade Access to alternative site and IT though a back-up system	Two hours for communication One day for alternative site Full service at alternative site in five working days Relocation in six weeks	Back at permanent site in six weeks

Annex 5H
Business continuity telephone cascade list

In the event of an emergency where communications are not possible through usual means, the senior management team will communicate with everyone through the department heads using the contact numbers below. The department heads will communicate with everyone in their group as denoted by group letter.

Name	Job description	Telephone numbers			Group
		Office	Mobile	Home	
Senior management					
					All
					All
					All
					All
					All
Heads of department					
					A
					B
					C
					D
					E
Team members					
					A
					A
					A
					B
					B
					B

Annex 5I

Complaints handling procedure (client version)

Our complaints policy

We are committed to providing a high quality legal service to all our clients. When something goes wrong, we need you to tell us about it. This will help us to improve our standards.

Our complaints procedure

If you have a complaint about our service or a bill that we have rendered or both, please contact us with the details.

The person to contact is [*name*], and [he/she] can be reached at:

[*Full postal address, direct line telephone number and email address*]

What will happen next?

1. We will send you a letter acknowledging receipt of your complaint within [*insert a realistic number*] days of us receiving the complaint, enclosing a copy of this procedure.
2. We will then investigate your complaint. This will normally involve passing your complaint to [*name*] who will review your file and speak to the member of staff who acted for you.
3. [*Name*] will then invite you to a meeting to discuss and hopefully resolve your complaint. This will be done within [*insert a realistic number*] days of sending you the acknowledgement letter.
4. Within [*insert a realistic number*] days of the meeting, [*name*] will write to you to confirm what took place and any solutions [he/she] has agreed with you.
5. If you do not want a meeting or it is not possible, [*name*] will send you a detailed written reply to your complaint, including [his/her] suggestions for resolving the matter, within [*insert a realistic number*] days of sending you the acknowledgement letter.
6. At this stage, if you are still not satisfied, you should contact us again and we will arrange for [another partner or someone unconnected with the matter at the practice to review the decision, [*or, for a sole practitioner:* [*name*] to review [his/her] own decision or [*insert appropriate alternative, such as review by another local solicitor or mediation*]]].
7. We will write to you within [*insert a realistic number*] days of receiving your request for a review, confirming our final position on your complaint and explaining our reasons.
8. If we have to change any of the timescales above, we will let you know and explain why.

9.   If you are still not satisfied, you can then contact the Legal Ombudsman at:

PO Box 6806
Wolverhampton
WV1 9WJ
Tel: 0300 555 0333 or 0121 245 3050
Email: enquiries@legalombudsman.org.uk

There are time limits within which complaints must be made to the Legal Ombudsman, as indicated below.

Generally speaking, your complaint should be made to the Ombudsman no later than 12 months from when the problem occurred or from when you should reasonably have become aware of the problem.

Additionally, you should make your complaint to the Ombudsman within six months of receiving a final response from us following the complaint that you have made to us.

Normally, your complaint needs to fall inside both rules if the Ombudsman is going to investigate it.

You also need to be aware that the Ombudsman only deals with complaints from the following:

(a)   an enterprise which, at the time that the complaint is made, is a micro-enterprise within the meaning of arts.1, 2(1) and (3) of the Annex to Commission Recommendation 2003/361/EC, as that Recommendation had effect at the date it was adopted;
(b)   a charity with an annual income net of tax of less than £1 million at the time at which the complainant refers the complaint to the respondent;
(c)   a club, association or organisation, the affairs of which are managed by its members or a committee or committees of its members, with an annual income net of tax of less than £1 million at the time at which the complainant refers the complaint to the respondent;
(d)   a trustee of a trust with an asset value of less than £1 million at the time at which the complainant refers the complaint to the respondent;
(e)   a personal representative of an estate of a person; or
(f)   a beneficiary of an estate of a person.

Annex 5J

Complaints monitoring report

This is a sample complaints report to partners/directors/managers. One line would be completed per complaint.

Period covered: ...... to ......

Internal procedure

Complaints reference	SRA complaints category	Date received	Department concerned	Time target met – acknowledge-ment (2 days) Yes/No	Outcome	Time target met – resolution (8 weeks)	Total amount paid in com-pensation	Total amount paid in fees waived/ refunded

Legal Ombudsman complaints

Complaints reference	SRA complaints category	Date received	Department concerned	Informal resolution outcome	Ombudsman decision outcome	Total amount paid in compensation	Total amount paid in fees waived/ refunded

Corrective action taken – comments:

Preventative action taken – comments:

Learning points from complaints in this period:

Annex 5K

Audit/file review form

Client name:	
File number:	
Fee earner:	
Practice area:	
Date:	
Reviewer:	

Checklist	Yes / No / n/a
File opening	
Has a conflict check been conducted and evidenced on file?	
AML/ID procedures complied with?	
Risk assessment completed?	
Client care and file management	
Compliant client care letter and terms and conditions/terms of business sent?	
Signed instructions received (if applicable)?	
Client accurately identified?	
Action plan agreed with client and correctly pursued?	
Client kept informed/updated on progress/costs updates issued?	
Any evidence of delay?	
File regularly reviewed?	
Attendance notes on file?	
Letters/phone calls answered promptly?	
Time recorded accurately?	
Key dates noted?	
File in good order and papers neatly filed?	
Any evidence of client complaint/dissatisfaction?	
Any positive feedback from client received?	
Financials	
WIP to be billed?	
Disbursements to be paid?	
Monies being held on client account for no reason?	
Estimate of costs exceeded?	

Corrective action to be completed within 28 days
1.
2.
3.
4.
5.

All corrective action complete/file review completed
1.
2.
3.
4.
5.

Signed off: _____

Date: _____

Annex 5L

File review corrective action form

Matter number:		**File review date:**	
Fee earner:		**Date:**	
Reviewer:			

Please see attached file review checklist. The following non-compliances have been identified:

Please explain what corrective action has been taken:

Signed:

Print name:

Date:

Please return to the reviewer within 28 days of the file review date for corrective action to be verified

Verification

Corrective action form received on:

I confirm that the necessary remedial action has/has not been completed.

Signed:

Print name:

Date:

Copy placed on matter file	☐	Copy to supervisor	☐	Copy to risk manager	☐

APPENDIX A

SRA Authorisation Rules 2011 (extracts)

Part 3: Conditions of authorisation

...

Rule 8: General conditions on authorisation

...

8.5 Compliance officers

(a) An authorised body must have suitable arrangements in place to ensure that its compliance officers are able to discharge their duties in accordance with these rules.

(b) Subject to Rule 8.5(h), an authorised body must at all times have an individual:

   (i) who is the sole practitioner, a manager or an employee of the authorised body;

   (ii) who is designated as its COLP;

   (iii) who is of sufficient seniority and in a position of sufficient responsibility to fulfil the role; and

   (iv) whose designation is approved by the SRA.

(c) The COLP of an authorised body must:

   (i) take all reasonable steps to:

      (A) ensure compliance with the terms and conditions of the authorised body's authorisation except any obligations imposed under the SRA Accounts Rules;

      (B) ensure compliance with any statutory obligations of the body, its managers, employees or interest holders or the sole practitioner in relation to the body's carrying on of authorised activities; and

      (C) record any failure so to comply and make such records available to the SRA on request; and

   (ii) in the case of a licensed body, as soon as reasonably practicable, report to the SRA any failure so to comply, provided that:

      (A) in the case of non-material failures, these shall be taken to have been reported as soon as reasonably practicable if they are reported to the SRA together with such other information as the SRA may require in accordance with Rule 8.7(a); and

(B) a failure may be material either taken on its own or as part of a pattern of failures so to comply.

(iii) in the case of a recognised body or recognised sole practice, as soon as reasonably practicable, report to the SRA any material failure so to comply (a failure may be material either taken on its own or as part of a pattern of failure so to comply).

(d) Subject to Rule 8.5(i), an authorised body must at all times have an individual:

(i) who is the sole practitioner, a manager or an employee of the authorised body;

(ii) who is designated as its COFA;

(iii) who is of sufficient seniority and in a position of sufficient responsibility to fulfil the role; and

(iv) whose designation is approved by the SRA.

(e) The COFA of an authorised body must:

(i) take all reasonable steps to:

(A) ensure that the body and its managers or the sole practitioner, and its employees comply with any obligations imposed upon them under the SRA Accounts Rules;

(B) record any failure so to comply and make such records available to the SRA on request; and

(ii) in the case of a licensed body, as soon as reasonably practicable, report to the SRA any failure so to comply, provided that:

(A) in the case of non-material failures, these shall be taken to have been reported as soon as reasonably practicable if they are reported to the SRA together with such other information as the SRA may require in accordance with Rule 8.7(a); and

(B) a failure may be material either taken on its own or as part of a pattern of failures so to comply.

(iii) in the case of a recognised body or recognised sole practice, as soon as reasonably practicable, report to the SRA any material failure so to comply (a failure may be material either taken on its own or as part of a pattern of failure so to comply).

(f) The SRA may approve an individual's designation as a COLP or COFA if it is satisfied, in accordance with Part 4, that the individual is a suitable person to carry out his or her duties.

(g) A designation of an individual as a COLP or COFA has effect only while the individual:

(i) consents to the designation;

(ii) in the case of a COLP:

(A) is not disqualified from acting as a HOLP; and

(B) is:

(I)   a lawyer of England and Wales;

(II)   an REL; or

(III)   registered with the BSB under Regulation 17 of the European Communities (Lawyer's Practice) Regulations 2000 (SI 2000/1119);

and is an authorised person in relation to one or more of the reserved legal activities which the body is authorised to carry on; and

(iii) in the case of a COFA, is not disqualified from acting as a HOFA.

(h)   An authorised body is not required to comply with Rule 8.5(b)(i) where the individual designated as its COLP:

(i)   has been approved by the SRA as a COLP for a related authorised body; and

(ii)   is a manager or employee of that related authorised body.

(i)   An authorised body is not required to comply with Rule 8.5(d)(i) where the individual designated as its COFA:

(i)   has been approved by the SRA as a COFA for a related authorised body; and

(ii)   is a manager or employee of that related authorised body.

...

Part 4: Approval of managers, owners and compliance officers

Rule 13: Application for approval

13.1 This Part governs the SRA's determination of applications for:

(a)   approval of an authorised body's managers and owners pursuant to Rule 8.6(a); and

(b)   approval of an authorised body's compliance officers, pursuant to Rule 8.5(b) and (d).

13.2 The SRA will deem a person to be approved as suitable to be a manager or owner of an authorised body under this Part if:

(a)   that person is:

(i)   a solicitor who holds a current practising certificate; or

(ii)   an authorised body;

(iii) an REL; or

(iv)   an RFL;

(b)   there is no condition on the person's practising certificate or authorisation as appropriate, preventing or restricting them from being a manager, owner or interest holder of an authorised body or being a sole practitioner;

(c) the SRA is notified on the prescribed form in advance of the person becoming a manager or owner of the authorised body; and

(d) the SRA has not withdrawn its approval of that person to be a manager or owner under Rule 17.

Rule 14: Approval process and production of information or documentation

14.1 An application for approval of a manager, owner or compliance officer may be made by an applicant body or an authorised body and must include evidence to satisfy the SRA that the candidate is suitable to be a manager, owner or compliance officer of the body, as appropriate.

14.2 The applicant body or authorised body, as appropriate, must:

(a) co-operate, and secure the co-operation of the candidate, to assist the SRA to obtain all information and documentation the SRA requires in order to determine the application;

(b) obtain all other information and documentation in relation to the candidate which the prescribed form requires the body to obtain and keep; and

(c) keep all information and documentation under (b) above for a period of not less than 6 years after the person concerned has ceased to be a manager, owner or compliance officer of the body.

14.3 [deleted]

14.4 The SRA's decision to approve or refuse approval must be notified in writing to the applicant body or authorised body as appropriate, as soon as possible.

14.5 The SRA may, at the time of granting its approval or at any time subsequently:

(a) approve the holding of a material interest in a licensed body subject to conditions in accordance with paragraphs 17, 28 or 33 of Schedule 13 to the LSA [Legal Services Act 2007]; and

(b) make its approval of a person to be an owner, manager or compliance officer of an authorised body subject to such conditions on the body's authorisation as it considers appropriate having regard to the criteria in Rule 9.

14.6 If the SRA proposes to object to a candidate becoming an owner of an applicant body or authorised body, or to approve such a person becoming an owner subject to conditions imposed under Rule 14.5(a) or (b), the SRA must:

(a) give the candidate and the body a warning notice which:

(i) specifies the SRA's intention to object or to impose conditions; and

(ii) states that any representations must be made to the SRA within the period of 28 days from the date of the notice; and

(b) consider any representations made to the SRA by the body and/or the candidate within the 28 day period in (a)(ii) above.

14.7 The SRA may issue a conditional approval or objection without a warning notice under Rule 14.6 if the application for approval has been made after the grant of authorisation and the SRA considers it necessary or desirable to dispense with the warning notice for the purpose of protecting any of the regulatory objectives.

14.8 The SRA may at any time require the production of information or documentation from:

(a) a person who has been approved as an owner, manager or compliance officer under this Part (including deemed approval under Rule 13.2 or 13.3);

(b) an authorised body of which that person is a manager, owner or compliance officer; or

(c) the body which originally obtained approval for that person and holds information and documentation under Rule 14.2(c);

in order to satisfy the SRA that the person met, meets, or continues to meet the criteria for approval.

Guidance notes

(i) See also the guidance notes to Rule 1 regarding ownership and material interest.

(ii) The SRA's notification "in writing" includes any form of written electronic communication normally used for business purposes, such as emails.

(iii) See also Regulation 7 of the SRA Practising Regulations under which the SRA has the power to impose conditions on a practising certificate or registration which restrict an individual's ability to be involved in an authorised body.

(iv) Specific provisions exist in the LSA about imposing conditions on the approval of owners of a licensed body:

(a) For the approval of ownership on an application for a licence, see paragraph 17 of Schedule 13 to the LSA. For the approval of ownership on a change of interests after a licence is issued, see paragraph 28 of that Schedule. These give the SRA the power to approve an owner's or a prospective owner's holding subject to conditions where the Rule 15 criteria are not met in relation to that investment, but only if the SRA considers that, if the conditions are complied with, it will be appropriate for the owner to hold the interest.

(b) For the imposition of conditions (or further conditions) on an existing ownership interest, see paragraph 33 of Schedule 13 to the LSA. This gives the SRA the power to impose conditions (or further conditions) on a person's holding of an interest, if the SRA is not satisfied that the Rule 15 criteria are met, or if the SRA is satisfied that a condition imposed under paragraphs 17, 28 or 33 of Schedule 13 (see above) on the person's holding of that interest has not been, or is not being, complied with. The SRA may only use the paragraph 33 power if it considers that, if the conditions are complied with, it will be appropriate for the owner to hold the interest without the approval requirements being met.

Rule 15: Criteria for approval

15.1 When considering whether a candidate should be approved to be a manager, owner or compliance officer of the body, as appropriate, the SRA will take into account the criteria set out in the SRA Suitability Test and any other relevant information.

Guidance notes

(i) As well as evidence about the candidate, the Suitability Test takes into account evidence about the honesty and integrity of a person that the candidate is related to, affiliated with, or acts together with where the SRA has reason to believe that that person may have an influence over the way in which the candidate will exercise their role.

(ii) Under paragraphs 19 and 20 of Schedule 13 to the LSA the SRA has the power, when dealing with an application for a licence, to object to the holding of an interest if it is not satisfied that the Rule 15 criteria are met in relation to that holding. The mechanism for objecting is set out in those paragraphs.

Rule 16: Effect of approval

16.1 Approval takes effect from the date of the decision unless otherwise stated and remains effective only if the candidate takes up the position for which he or she has been approved within the period specified in the notice of approval.

16.2 Subject to Rule 16.1, approval continues until:

(a) it is withdrawn by the SRA; or

(b) the approved person ceases to be a manager, interest holder, COLP or COFA of the authorised body, as appropriate.

Guidance note

(i) The period specified in the notice of approval in Rule 16.1 will normally be 90 days although may be varied in individual cases.

Rule 17: Withdrawal of approval

17.1 Where the SRA has granted an approval of a person to be a manager, owner or compliance officer of a body (including a deemed approval under Rule 13.2 or Rule 13.3), it may subsequently withdraw that approval if:

(a) it is not satisfied that an approved person met or meets the criteria for approval in Rule 15;

(b) it is satisfied that a condition imposed on the body's authorisation under Rule 14.5 has not been, or is not being complied with;

(c) it is satisfied that the approved person has breached a duty or obligation imposed upon them in or under the SRA's regulatory arrangements or any enactments; or

(d) information or documentation is not promptly supplied in response to a request made under Rule 14.8.

17.2 Where withdrawal of approval relates to a director of a company, the SRA may set separate dates for that individual ceasing to be a director and disposing of his or her shares.

Rule 18: *Temporary emergency approvals for compliance officers*

18.1 If an authorised body ceases to have a COLP or COFA whose designation has been approved by the SRA (including deemed approval under Rule 13.3), the authorised body must immediately and in any event within seven days:

(a) notify the SRA;
(b) designate the sole practitioner, another manager or employee to replace its previous COLP or COFA, as appropriate; and
(c) make an application to the SRA for temporary approval of the new COLP or COFA, as appropriate.

18.2 The SRA may grant a temporary approval under this rule if:

(a) it is satisfied that the authorised body could not reasonably have commenced an application for approval of designation in advance of the non-compliance; and
(b) on the face of the application and any other information immediately before the SRA, there is no evidence suggesting that the new compliance officer is not suitable to carry out the duties imposed on them under these rules.

18.3 Temporary approval under this rule:

(a) may be granted initially for 28 days;
(b) may be granted to have effect from the date the body ceases to have a COLP or COFA whose designation has been approved;
(c) may be extended in response to a reasonable request by the authorised body;
(d) must be extended pending determination of a substantive application for approval commenced in accordance with Rule 18.4;
(e) may be granted or extended subject to such conditions on the authorised body's authorisation as the SRA thinks fit, having regard to the criteria in Rule 9;
(f) has effect only while the criteria in Rule 8.5(g) are met;
(g) if granted, cannot prejudice the discretion of the SRA to refuse a substantive application for approval of designation or to impose any conditions on that approval; and
(h) in exceptional circumstances, and for reasonable cause, may be withdrawn at any time.

18.4 If granted temporary approval under Rule 18.3 above for its designation of a new COLP or COFA, the authorised body must:

(a) designate a permanent COLP or COFA, as appropriate; and

(b) submit a substantive application for approval of that designation under Rule 13;

before the expiry of the temporary approval or any extension of that approval by the SRA.

APPENDIX B

SRA Suitability Test 2011

Introduction to the Suitability Test

Preamble

Authority: Made on 17 June 2011 by the Solicitors Regulation Authority Board under sections 28, 79 and 80 of the Solicitors Act 1974 with the approval of the Legal Services Board under paragraph 19 of Schedule 4 to the Legal Services Act 2007

Date: These regulations came into force on 6 October 2011

Replacing: The SRA guidelines on the assessment of character and suitability

Applicability: Students and trainee solicitors under the SRA Training Regulations;

Qualified lawyers under the QLTSR;

Those seeking admission as solicitors under the Admission Regulations, fulfilling the duties under section 3 of the Solicitors Act 1974;

Those seeking to become authorised role holders in accordance with rules 8.5 and 8.6 of the SRA Authorisation Rules and regulation 4.8 of the SRA Practising Regulations;

Those seeking restoration to the roll of solicitors under regulation 8 of the Solicitors Keeping of the Roll Regulations 2011.

Overview

Outcomes-focused regulation concentrates on providing positive outcomes which when achieved will benefit and protect *clients* and the public. We must ensure that any individual admitted as a *solicitor* has, and maintains, the level of honesty, integrity and the professionalism expected by the public and other stakeholders and professionals, and does not pose a risk to the public or the profession.

The Suitability Test will apply the same high standards to all those seeking admission or restoration to the roll as a *solicitor*, as well as legally qualified and non-legally qualified applicants for roles in authorised bodies as *authorised role holders*.

The test is the same for non-solicitors as they will be working within the profession and must meet the same high standards that the general public expect of *solicitors*. This document is intended to make it clear to *you* what this standard is in terms of *your* character, suitability, fitness and propriety.

No applicant has the automatic right of admission, restoration or authorisation and it will always be for *you* to discharge the burden of satisfying suitability under this test. Any application that requires *us* to be satisfied as to character, suitability, fitness and propriety will be determined by reference to this test.

The Principles

The Suitability Test forms part of the Handbook, in which the 10 mandatory *Principles* are all-pervasive. They apply to all those *we* regulate and to all aspects of practice.

You must:

1   uphold the rule of law and the proper administration of justice;
2   act with integrity;
3   not allow *your* independence to be compromised;
4   act in the best interests of each *client*;
5   provide a proper standard of service to *your clients*;
6   behave in a way that maintains the trust the public places in *you* and in the provision of legal services;
7   comply with *your* legal and regulatory obligations and deal with *your* regulators and ombudsmen in an open, timely and co-operative manner;
8   run *your* business or carry out *your* role in the business effectively and in accordance with proper governance and sound financial and risk management principles;
9   run *your* business or carry out *your* role in the business in a way that encourages equality of opportunity and respect for diversity; and
10 protect *client money* and *assets*.

Outcomes

The outcomes which apply to this test are as follows:

O(SB1) if *you* are a *solicitor*, *you* are of the required standard of *character and suitability*;
O(SB2) if *you* are an *authorised role holder*, *you* are fit and proper; and
O(SB3) *you* act so that *clients*, and the wider public, have confidence that O(SB1) has been demonstrated.

The outcomes, and the criteria that flow from them, apply to all those who are intending to become *solicitors* – i.e. students, *trainee solicitors*, and qualified lawyers from other jurisdictions seeking qualification via transfer – at the point of *student enrolment*, admission, and throughout the pre-qualification period. They also apply to *compliance officers*, *owners*, and/or *managers* at the point of and throughout their period of authorisation, and for former *solicitors* seeking restoration to the roll.

Interpretation and definitions

1   The SRA Handbook Glossary 2012 shall apply and, unless the context otherwise requires:

(a) all italicised terms shall be defined; and
(b) all terms shall be interpreted;

in accordance with the *Glossary*.

2   In this test, the reference in the preamble to those seeking to become *authorised role holders* in accordance with rules 8.5 and 8.6 of the *SRA Authorisation Rules*, fulfilling the duties under Sections 89, 90, 91 and 92 of the *LSA* shall have no effect until such time as the Society is designated as a licensing authority under Part 1 of Schedule 10 to the *LSA*.

3   This test shall not apply to licensed bodies until such time as the Society is designated as a licensing authority under Part 1 of Schedule 10 to the *LSA* and all definitions shall be construed accordingly.

4   Part 2 of this test shall have no effect until such time as the Society is designated as a licensing authority under Part 1 of Schedule 10 to the *LSA*.

Part 1: Basic requirements

If *you* are applying for *student enrolment*, admission or restoration to the roll, *you* must comply with Part 1. If *you* are applying for authorisation as an *authorised role holder* then *you* must comply with Part 1 and Part 2.

When considering any application under this test, *we* will take the following actions:

1: Criminal offences

1.1   Unless there are exceptional circumstances, *we* will refuse *your* application if *you* have been convicted by a *court* of a criminal offence:

(a) for which *you* received a custodial or suspended sentence;
(b) involving dishonesty, fraud, perjury and/or bribery;
(c) specifically in relation to which *you* have been included on the Violent and Sex Offender Register;
(d) associated with obstructing the course of justice;
(e) which demonstrated behaviour showing signs of *discrimination* towards others;
(f) associated with terrorism;
(g) which was racially aggravated;

(h) which was motivated by any of the 'protected' characteristics defined within the Equality Act 2010;

(i) which in *our* judgement is so serious as to prevent *your student enrolment*, admission as a *solicitor*, or approval as an *authorised role holder*; and/or

(j) *you* have been convicted by a *court* of more than one criminal offence.

Guidance note

(i) The provisions in 1.1(a) will not be relevant to entities because *bodies corporate*, and other unincorporated bodies and bodies of persons, cannot themselves receive custodial sentences.

1.2 *We* are more likely than not to refuse *your* application if *you* have:

(a) been convicted by a *court* of a criminal offence not falling within 1.1 above but which has an impact on *your character and suitability*;

(b) been included on the Violent and Sex Offender Register but in relation to *your* inclusion on the Register, *you* have not been convicted by a *court* of a criminal offence; and/or

(c) accepted a caution for an offence involving dishonesty.

1.3 *We* may refuse *your* application if *you* have:

(a) received a local warning from the police;

(b) accepted a caution from the police for an offence not involving dishonesty;

(c) received a Penalty Notice for Disorder (PND) from the police;

(d) received a final warning or reprimand from the police (youths only); and/ or

(e) received a referral order from the *courts* (youths only).

Guidance note

(i) Where a criminal conviction, warning, simple caution, PND and/or inclusion on the Violent and Sex Offender Register has been disclosed, *we* will not look behind the decision made by the police or the finding made by a *court*. However, *we* will take into account material such as sentencing remarks and any other independent information. See also Section 7 Evidence.

(ii) *You* should disclose details of any criminal charge(s) *you* may be facing. *We* will not determine *your* application until *you* can confirm that the charge(s) has/have either been dropped or the outcome of *your* case is known.

(iii) Cautions and local warnings issued by the police may be subsequently recorded on the Police National Computer (PNC) and these will be shown on a PNC printout, which *you* may be required to submit to *us*.

(iv) Police can only issue a caution if there is evidence that *you* are guilty of an offence and if *you* admit that *you* committed the offence. Therefore, by accepting a caution, please bear in mind that *you* are making an admission of guilt.

(v)   On Penalty Notices for Disorder no admission of guilt is required, and by paying the penalty, a recipient discharges liability for conviction for the offence – however, *you* should still disclose such matters as *we* will need to consider them.

(vi) Serious motoring offences that result in a criminal conviction must be disclosed. Motoring offences that do not result in a criminal conviction do not need to be disclosed.

2: *Disclosure*

2.1   All material information relating to *your* application must be disclosed. Failure to disclose material information will be treated as prima facie evidence of dishonest behaviour.

2.2   *You* must disclose any matters that have occurred in the *UK* and/or overseas.

Guidance note

(i)   *You* should bear in mind that Regulation 35 of the *SRA Training Regulations* Part 1 – Qualification Regulations requires all those seeking admission as *solicitors* to apply for a standard disclosure from the Criminal Records Bureau (CRB). *We* will also perform a PNC check at the *student enrolment* stage and have reciprocal arrangements with other jurisdictions in order to gather similar information on lawyers from other countries.

(ii) If *you* are seeking approval as an *authorised role holder*, *you* should bear in mind that Rule 14 of the *SRA Authorisation Rules* allows *us* to seek other information relating to *your* application and this would normally include CRB disclosure.

(iii) It is therefore highly likely that matters will come to light.

3: *Behaviour not compatible with that expected of a prospective solicitor or authorised role holder*

3.1   Unless there are exceptional circumstances *we* will refuse *your* application if *you* have:

(a)   been responsible for behaviour:

(i) which is dishonest;
(ii) which is violent;
(iii) where there is evidence of *discrimination* towards others;

(b)   misused *your* position to obtain pecuniary advantage;
(c)   misused *your* position of trust in relation to vulnerable people; and/or
(d)   been responsible for other forms of behaviour which demonstrate that *you* cannot be relied upon to discharge *your* regulatory duties as a *solicitor* or *authorised role holder*.

4: Assessment offences

4.1 Unless there are exceptional circumstances *we* will refuse *your* application if *you* have committed and/or have been adjudged by an education establishment to have committed a deliberate assessment offence which amounts to plagiarism or cheating to gain an advantage for *yourself* or others.

Guidance note

(i) Exceptional circumstances may include where the finding does not amount to cheating or dishonesty, e.g. incorrect referencing, or failure to attribute correctly, in an essay or paper.

5: Financial evidence

5.1 Unless there are exceptional circumstances *we* will refuse *your* application if:

(a) there is evidence that *you* cannot manage *your* finances properly and carefully;

(b) there is evidence that *you* have deliberately sought to avoid responsibility for *your* debts; and/or

(c) there is evidence of dishonesty in relation to the management of *your* finances.

5.2 If *you* have been declared bankrupt, entered into any individual voluntary arrangements (IVA) or have had a County Court Judgement issued against *you* it will raise a presumption that there has been evidence that *you* cannot manage *your* finances properly and carefully.

Guidance note

(i) The following might help to establish confidence in *your* ability to run *your* business/carry out *your* role in the business effectively and in accordance with proper governance and sound financial and risk management principles:

(a) the bankruptcy/IVA/County Court Judgement occurred many years ago and there is evidence of subsequent sound financial management and conduct to show that creditors have been repaid;

(b) *you* were affected by exceptional circumstances beyond *your* control which *you* could not have reasonably foreseen.

6: Regulatory history

6.1 Unless there are exceptional circumstances *we* will refuse *your* application if *you*:

(a) have been made the subject of a serious disciplinary finding, sanction or action by a regulatory body and/or any *court* or other body hearing appeals in relation to disciplinary or regulatory findings;

(b) have failed to disclose information to a regulatory body when required to do so, or have provided false or misleading information;

(c) have significantly breached the requirements of a regulatory body;

(d) have been refused registration by a regulatory body; and/or

(e) have failed to comply with the reasonable requests of a regulatory body.

6.2 *We* may refuse *your* application if *you* have been rebuked, reprimanded or received a warning about *your* conduct by a regulatory body, unless there are exceptional circumstances.

Guidance note

(i) "Regulatory body" includes *us* and the Solicitors Disciplinary Tribunal, approved regulators under the Legal Services Act 2007, as well as any other body responsible for regulation of a profession.

(ii) *You* should disclose details of any disciplinary proceeding(s) or investigation(s) *you* may be facing. *We* will not determine *your* application until *you* can confirm that the matter(s) has/have either been dropped or the outcome of *your* case is known.

7: *Evidence*

7.1 To help *us* consider an application where a disclosure has been made, *you* should include the following evidence, where relevant:

(a) at least one independent report relating to the event(s), such as sentencing remarks following a criminal conviction;

(b) references from at least two independent professional people (of which one should preferably be from an employer or tutor) who know *you* well and are familiar with the matters being considered;

(c) evidence of any rehabilitation (e.g. probation reports, references from employers and/or tutors);

(d) documentary evidence in support of *your* case and where possible, an independent corroboration of *your* account of the event(s);

(e) *your* attitude towards the event(s);

(f) the extent to which *you* were aware of the rules and procedures governing the reference of material, or the use of group work or collaborative material;

(g) the extent to which *you* could reasonably have been expected to realise that the offence did not constitute legitimate academic practice;

(h) credit check information (in the relevant circumstances); and/or

(i) actions *you* have taken to clear any debts, satisfy any judgements and manage *your* finances.

7.2 The onus is on *you* to provide any evidence *you* consider necessary and/or appropriate. However, should *we* consider that *you* have provided insufficient evidence, *we* reserve the right to carry out *our* own investigation and/or refuse the application if further evidence is not forthcoming.

8: Rehabilitation

8.1 It is for *you* to demonstrate that *you* have undergone successful rehabilitation, where relevant. The individual circumstances *you* put forward must be weighed against the public interest and the need to safeguard members of the public and maintain the reputation of the profession. However, *we* will consider each application on its own merits.

8.2 If the Rehabilitation of Offenders Act 1974 (Exceptions) Order 1975 (as amended) is applicable to *your* occupation, profession or role, *you* must declare all convictions and cautions, even if they are deemed to be spent in accordance with the Act.

8.3 In accordance with paragraph 2 above (disclosure), if *you* fall within the Rehabilitation of Offenders Act 1974 (Exceptions) Order 1975 and *you* fail to disclose information about convictions and/or cautions for criminal offences, whether they are spent or unspent, *we* will consider this as amounting to prima facie evidence of dishonest behaviour.

Guidance note

(i) The provisions of the Rehabilitation of Offenders Act 1974 (as amended) and the Rehabilitation of Offenders Act 1974 (Exceptions) Order 1975 (as amended) will be taken into account by *us* in considering any application *you* make.

(ii) If *you* fall within the Rehabilitation of Offenders Act 1974 (Exceptions) Order 1975 (as amended), the fact that the conviction is spent, and the time that has passed since the conviction was given, together with any other material circumstances will be taken into account by *us* when determining any application made by *you*.

(iii) A period of rehabilitation, particularly after *we* have decided to refuse *your* application, will not in itself result in automatic admission/authorisation. *We* need *you* to show, through a period of good behaviour, that *you* have taken steps to rehabilitate *yourself* by *your* own volition.

Part 2: Additional requirements to become authorised under the SRA Authorisation Rules

9: All applicants must comply with Part 1

9.1 Under this test, when considering any application by an individual seeking to become an *authorised role holder*, all of the tests set out in Part 1 will apply in addition to this Part.

10: Additional requirements

10.1 Unless there are exceptional circumstances *we* may refuse *your* application if:

(a)   *you* have been removed from the office of trustee for a charity by an order imposed by the Charities Act 1993;

(b)   *you* have been removed and/or disqualified as a company director;

(c)   any body corporate of which *you* are/were a *manager* or *owner* has been the subject of a winding up order, an administrative order or an administrative receivership, or has otherwise been wound up or put into administration in circumstances of insolvency;

(d)   *you* have a previous conviction which is now spent for a criminal offence relating to bankruptcy, IVAs or other circumstances of insolvency;

(e)   *you* are a corporate person/entity subject to a relevant insolvency event defined in rule 1.2 of the *SRA Authorisation Rules*;

(f)   *you* are a corporate person/entity and other matters that call *your* fitness and propriety into question are disclosed or come to light;

(g)   *you* have committed an offence under the Companies Act 2006; and/or

(h)   *we* have evidence reflecting on the honesty and integrity of a person *you* are related to, affiliated with, or act together with where *we* have reason to believe that the person may have an influence over the way in which *you* will exercise *your authorised role*.

Guidance note

(i)   The provisions of the Rehabilitation of Offenders Act 1974 (as amended) and the Rehabilitation of Offenders Act 1974 (Exceptions) Order 1975 (as amended) do not apply to corporate persons/entities. Therefore, corporate convictions cannot become spent, so if *you* are a corporate person/entity *you* must disclose any and all matters in *your* application.

(ii)   Other matters under 10.1(f) include but are not limited to debts, corporate criminal matters, Companies Act transgressions such as late submission of accounts, and taking steps without submitting proper documents to Companies House.

APPENDIX C

Further guidance

Further guidance available online at the time of printing of this toolkit:

SRA website

- SRA Handbook

  www.sra.org.uk/solicitors/handbook/welcome.page

- FAQs: Compliance officers for legal practice (COLPs) and compliance officers for finance and administration (COFAs)

  www.sra.org.uk/solicitors/colp-cofa/help/faqs.page

- SRA Risk Outlooks

  www.sra.org.uk/risk/risk-outlook.page

- Compliance News

  www.sra.org.uk/solicitors/colp-cofa/resources/compliance-news.page

Law Society website

- Summary of the SRA Handbook reporting requirements

  www.lawsociety.org.uk/support-services/advice/articles/sra-reporting-requirements/

- Compliance officer FAQs

  www.lawsociety.org.uk/support-services/advice/articles/compliance-officer-faqs/

- Law Society's practice notes

  - Outcomes-focused regulation: overview

    www.lawsociety.org.uk/support-services/advice/practice-notes/ofr-overview/

  - Compliance officers

    www.lawsociety.org.uk/support-services/advice/practice-notes/compliance-officers/

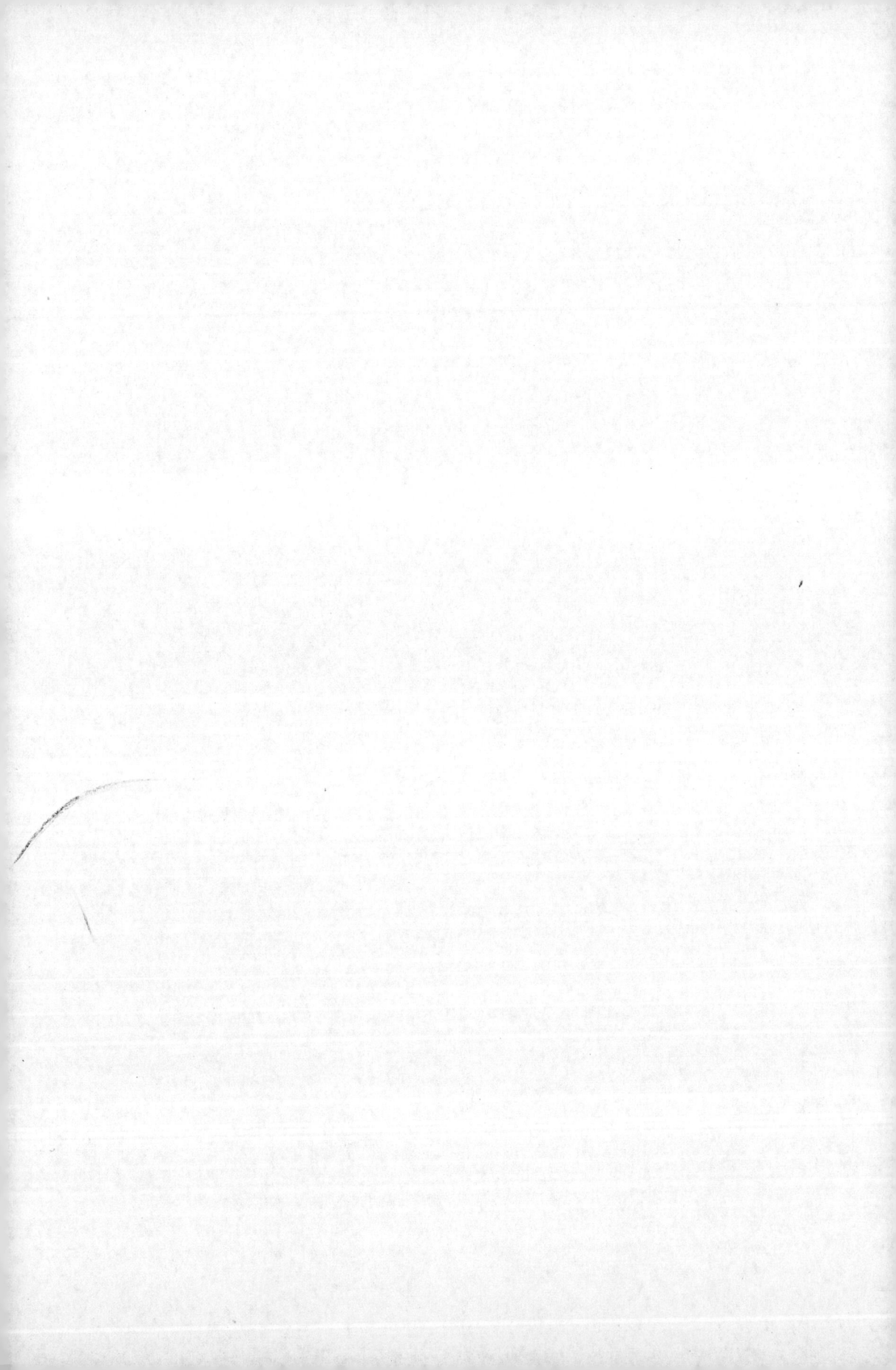